Chrystal has written a book that inspired me to desire a closer walk with God while giving me a sure guide to become more consistent in seeking Him through prayer. I know you will treasure this book.

—**SALLY CLARKSON,** author, blogger, podcaster;
sallyclarkson.com

Let Chrystal Evans Hurst take you on an unforgettable journey of prayer. You'll be challenged to dig deeper into areas you usually run from, inspired to take a second look at the things you take for granted, and most of all, invited to experience a new level of freedom in prayer. With every step, Chrystal reminds us that the goal is not perfection but simply opening ourselves to God's limitless love.

—**JEN FULWILER,** standup comic, mom of six,
author of bestselling *Your Blue Flame*

Chrystal takes you by the hand like a close friend and walks alongside you, as guide and encourager, into a richer prayer life. You'll find the prompts accessible, biblical, and fun. So join Chrystal on a twenty-eight-day journey that may change you in ways you never imagined.

—**MARGARET FEINBERG,** author of *Taste and See: Discovering God among Butchers, Bakers, and Fresh Food Makers*

To anyone who's longed for deeper connection and more intentional conversations with God, this twenty-eight-day prayer journey is more than a guide, it is a tool to use again and again. I felt a renewed passion in my relationship with God just as I would attending twenty-eight days of therapeutic marriage counseling restoring a love I didn't even know lacked attention and affection. Chrystal's powerful prayer prompts for morning, noon, and night offer a language and space that, trapped in stagnant intentionality, I had often longed to make.

—**CANDACE PAYNE,** author, speaker,
viral sensation, joy evangelist

One of the most important ways we can spend our lives is in prayer. In Chrystal's newest book, she gives us twenty-eight days of easy-to-pray prayer prompts to help us develop the discipline of daily personal prayer. If you want a friend to come alongside you and encourage you to develop this life-changing habit, pick up this book and watch how your prayer life is transformed. You're only twenty-eight days away!

—**ANGELA PERRITT,** founder and director of
Love God Greatly Women's Ministry

Let me let you in on a secret. Whenever I need wisdom, I know who to go to, and Chrystal Hurst is one of my wisdom people. Whatever she writes, I will read. Whatever she says, I listen. Because I know she listens to God. This twenty-eight-day prayer journey is powerful, life-giving, and life-changing. I am guessing I'll go on this journey at least once a year.

—**NICKI KOZIARZ,** bestselling author and
speaker with Proverbs 31 Ministries

If you are anything like me, the times I need to be praying the most are the times that it is hardest for me to settle my heart and connect with God. And sometimes, when I'm stuck, I just need someone who loves me to take me by the hand and show me which way to go. In this book, Chrystal is that loving friend who can not only guide you in the habit and rhythm of prayer but also help you discover (or rediscover) its power in your life.

—**KATHI LIPP,** speaker and bestselling author of *The Husband Project, Clutter Free,* and *Ready for Anything*

This is not "just another prayer journal." My friend, Chrystal, has given us a much needed gift. This is an intimate journey we all need to embark on. Whether you are just starting out on your journey with God, or you've been walking with him for a while, the next twenty-eight days will refresh you and remind you of the transforming, reassuring, gift of prayer. Chrystal offers each of us an opportunity to reap the rewards of her personal journey back to intimacy with Christ.

This is more than a book to read, it's an experience to be had—and worth having two or three times over. As a spouse, it will transform your marriage; as a leader, it will transform your church; as a parent, it will transform your family; and as a Christ follower, it will beckon your heart to transform your personal world and the world around you.

Chrystal invites us on a journey "to become addicted to your time with Jesus." She provides a gentle but passionate reminder that our prayer lives can always be deeper and more persistent. You can start to change that today.

—**JADA EDWARDS,** Creative Services Director,
One Community Church; author, *The Captive Mind*

My heart needed this book! In a discipline with which so many of us struggle, Chrystal Evans Hurst leads us toward growth with strength and simplicity. I've been praying for decades, but I found myself built up in places that I didn't know were weak and revitalized in areas with solid foundations. Chrystal's step-by-step guidance leads us to a new habit of praying through the day every day.

—**AMY CARROLL,** speaker and writer, Proverbs 31
Ministries; author, *Breaking Up with Perfect* and *Exhale*

Prayer is the foundation upon which to build a dynamic and healthy spiritual life. So what does it take to develop a fruitful prayer life? Chrystal Hurst Evans knows that the intimacy, power, and purpose we seek are best birthed through a lifestyle of prayer. In this book, Chrystal urges us to boldly connect with God in a personal and intimate way that will release His power and nurture our souls. I recommend it for everyone who longs to experience the power and presence of God on a daily basis.

—**JAN GREENWOOD,** Equip Pastor, Gateway
Church, and founder of Brave Strong Girl

Uncompromising belonging, inspired understanding. I feel this way after only a few minutes of in-person conversation with Chrystal. So it makes sense that this book would awaken me to God in such a similar way. This book will not only change the way you think about prayer, it will create a personal and sensory experience for you to enter into heaven, agreeing with God in real time and in light of your eternal sense of self. Most of us feel insecure and unwise in our daily lives. My own prayer life often feels defeated before I begin, simply because I don't have a plan to believe God more today than I did yesterday. This book is our plan of attack through the posture of promise. Here, we are given weapons to fight against our real enemy. Here, we see our full acceptance through the mind of Christ. Thank you, Chrystal, for this offering. It is a force. I will read it over and over again.

—**KASEY VAN NORMAN,** professional
counselor, author, and teacher

Chrystal is one of the most insightful women I know. She doesn't just ingest an idea. She circles it, ruminates on it, offers it to God, and consistently uses what she finds to benefit others. My life has been enriched by her mental strength and wise counsel, and I have no doubt that yours will as well.

—**JONATHAN PITTS,** author and president
of For Girls Like You ministries

THE 28-DAY

Prayer

JOURNEY

A DAILY GUIDE TO CONVERSATIONS WITH GOD

CHRYSTAL EVANS HURST

ZONDERVAN
BOOKS

ZONDERVAN BOOKS

The 28-Day Prayer Journey
Copyright © 2020 by Chrystal Evans Hurst

Requests for information should be addressed to:
Zondervan, 3900 *Sparks Dr. SE, Grand Rapids, Michigan 49546*

Zondervan titles may be purchased in bulk for educational, business, fundraising, or sales promotional use. For information, please email SpecialMarkets@Zondervan.com.

ISBN 978-0-310-36115-2 (audio)

Library of Congress Cataloging-in-Publication Data

Names: Hurst, Chrystal Evans, author. Title: The 28-day prayer journey : a daily guide to
    conversations with God / Chrystal Evans Hurst.
Other titles: Twenty-eight day prayer journey
Description: Grand Rapids : Zondervan, 2020. | Summary: "For anyone who longs for a
    consistent prayer life yet struggles with distractions, doubts, or knowing where to start,
    bestselling writer and beloved speaker Chrystal Evans Hurst offers The 28-Day Prayer
    Journey, a simple and heartfelt guide to intentional and intimate conversations with a
    loving God"-- Provided by publisher.
Identifiers: LCCN 2020018416 (print) | LCCN 2020018417 (ebook) | ISBN 9780310361138
    (trade paperback) | ISBN 9780310361145 (ebook)
Subjects: LCSH: Prayer--Christianity. | Meditations. | Spiritual journals--Authorship. | Diaries--
    Authorship--Religious aspects--Christianity.
Classification: LCC BV215 .H87 2020 (print) | LCC BV215 (ebook) | DDC 248.3/2--dc23
LC record available at https://lccn.loc.gov/2020018416
LC ebook record available at https://lccn.loc.gov/2020018417

Cover design: *Studio Gearbox*
Cover illustration: *Ullithemrg / Shutterstock*
Interior design: *Kait Lamphere*

Printed in the United States of America

20 21 22 23 24 25 26 27 28 29 30 31 32 /LSC/ 15 14 13 12 11 10 9 8 7 6 5 4

For my cousin Clarise

When I think of the powerful prayers our grandmother Eleen
and our aunt Elizabeth prayed for all of us, I think of you.
Your commitment to prioritizing prayer
reminds me to do the same.

CONTENTS

Introduction 1

Week 1 5
Week 2 49
Week 3 97
Week 4 145
Creating Your Prayer Plan: Day 29 and Beyond 187

Prayer Directory... 191
    Prayer for Joy and Contentment........................ 192
    Prayer for Hard Days 192
    Prayer for Wisdom 193
    Prayer for Marriage.................................. 193
    Prayer for Singleness 194
    Prayer for Grief 195
    Prayer for Forgiving Another Person 196
    Prayer for the Desire to Pray or to Read God's Word...... 196
    Prayer for Self-Control............................... 197
    Prayer for Rest...................................... 198
    Prayer for Friendship 198
    Prayer for Community 199
Praise Prompts 200
Books on Prayer 209
Acknowledgments...211

INTRODUCTION

A few years ago, I decided to put together a 28-Day Prayer Challenge on Instagram. I'd been feeling guilty about my lack of consistent and fervent prayer, so I figured I'd commit to providing twenty-eight days' worth of prayer prompts to hold me accountable to pray and to encourage others to do the same.

While I knew the basic format for prayer, as Jesus modeled in Matthew 6 (what we commonly call The Lord's Prayer), I made up the content, one day at a time, throughout the challenge. As I paused to think about what I needed to talk to God about, I shared those thoughts with others and encouraged them to do the same.

I honestly didn't think I'd finish.

I was afraid I'd fall off the wagon and fail myself and everyone doing it with me.

But I didn't. I finished the challenge and invigorated my prayer life by doing so.

Praying intentionally—bit by bit, day by day—made the idea of regular, consistent prayer much less formidable. I did it because one day at a time seemed *doable*.

This book is born of that challenge and is written with the same goal in mind. I want you to commit to prayer, but I also want you to view this commitment as doable.

And if you skip a day (or a few days), that's okay! Lord knows I have done the same. But don't give up. Pick up where you left off. Ignore the day of the week if you have to and just pray. Keep going. Perfection is not required. Simply show up to talk to God knowing that He wants to talk to you.

This book gives you three prompts a day—morning, afternoon, and evening. The first four days of the week, we'll cover the basic tenets of prayer:

1. Monday: **P**raise and Thanksgiving (offering gratitude to God)
2. Tuesday: **R**epent (seeking forgiveness from God)
3. Wednesday: **A**sk (presenting your requests to God)
4. Thursday: **Y**ield (surrendering to God)

While we'll be praying for others throughout the week, during the last three days we'll be more intentional about moving outside of ourselves and toward our families, friends, community, and world.

5. Friday: Family and friends
6. Saturday: Saturday challenge
7. Sunday: Sabbath prayers

As you pray, I will gently lead you through each tenet so that you can understand and think deeply about it. Then, slowly but surely, we'll put it all together.

The goal is for you to keep this little book with you for twenty-eight days. Glance at it three times a day so that you are prompted to talk to God every morning, afternoon, and evening.

If you think you might forget, try doing it every time you eat. Grabbing a bite? Open up the book. Or try setting an alarm on your watch or phone (but don't dismiss the reminder until you've picked up the book!).

After making this twenty-eight-day journey twice, I know one thing for sure: slow and steady wins the race. This method will help you form new habits if you'll commit to it, little by little, one day at a time, for the next four weeks.

If you want to learn more about having a dynamic connection with God through prayer, I encourage you to check out the video curriculum and study guide for *The 28-Day Prayer Journey*. These complementary materials are a perfect way to learn more about the powerful impact talking to God can have on your life. To get all the details and help for using the study along with the book or for studying with a friend or your small group, go to:

www.ChrystalEvansHurst.com/pray

My prayer is that God will become more real to you than ever before as you spend time abiding with Him.

It's possible. How do I know? Because it's happened for me.

Week 1

DAY 1 · *Monday*

PRAISE AND THANKSGIVING

*Today we are praising and thanking God
for His spiritual work in our hearts.*

MORNING MEDITATION

Sometimes when we go to God in prayer, we do it with a big laundry list of what we want God to do for us! (Not me, of course. Other people.) And thankfully, God is gracious to hear and receive our prayers for what we need and want.

But the first day of our prayer journey, and the first day of each prayer week, is dedicated to praising and thanking God. When we praise God, we adore Him for who He is. When we thank God, we express our gratitude for what He has done. Rather than beginning with ourselves, our prayers of praise begin with God. If God never did another thing for us, these are the reasons we would still love, admire, and honor Him.

Here's the real deal: when you praise God, you don't need a bunch of religious fanfare. Just tell Him what you think about Him that's good. Compliment Him like you would compliment a friend. Seriously, it's as simple as taking a moment—any moment during your day—and telling God what you know to be true about Him.

And thanking God is pretty simple too.

Do you remember a few years back when it became "the thing" to keep a gratitude journal? Perhaps you've already discovered for yourself how powerful it can be to choose gratitude every day. Research has demonstrated that we can transform our attitudes—toward God, toward others, and even toward ourselves—when we practice gratitude. When we slow down to pay attention to our lives—spiritually, physically, relationally—we notice all that God has provided for us. And we have the opportunity to give God thanks.

Today, we're going to thank God for what He has done for us spiritually. And over the next several weeks, we'll thank God for what we've been given physically and socially. We'll even thank God for the challenges we face. (Stay tuned to learn more!) This morning, thank God for all that He has done, spiritually, in *you*. (Later on today, you'll pray for others.)

PRAYER PROMPT

Dear God, thank You for my salvation and my life with You.

- If you can recall the particular moment of your salvation, give God thanks for all that led you to that moment.
- If God gave you a family—parents, siblings, grandparents, aunts and uncles—who nourished your faith as a child, thank God for each of them.
- If your spirit was nurtured in a community of faith, give God thanks for all those in Christ's body who cared for you and loved you to faith in Jesus.

This morning, give God thanks for your relationship with Him through Jesus.

AFTERNOON REFLECTION

Today you're thanking God for all that He's done for you and others spiritually. This morning you thanked God for your salvation, and this afternoon I want you to thank God for what He's done in the lives of others: loving and redeeming and guiding them.

One of the people whose faith I thank God for is my mom. Her faithful walk with Jesus not only shaped me but also formed faith in my sister and my brothers. As we watched her depend on God—in good times and in trying times—we learned what it looks like to trust God and walk with Him. God used my mother's spiritual life in our lives, and in the lives of so many others, and so I thank God for her faith in Him.

- Maybe you had grandparents or parents whose faith was a solid rock for your family. Thank God for their faith.
- Maybe you had a sibling or some other peer who shepherded you by taking you to youth group or summer camp, where you met Jesus. Thank God for their faith.
- Maybe there's a pastor or other spiritual leader who invested in you and brought you near to God. Thank God for their faith.
- Maybe you see faith forming in the life of your child, a niece or nephew, or another young person. Thank God for their faith.

This afternoon, give God thanks for His grace in calling others to Himself.

EVENING INSPIRATION

In his letter to the Romans, Paul addresses the hope of believers. They've received spiritual salvation, but they're waiting for the redemption of their *bodies*. He explains, "But hope that is seen is no hope at all. Who hopes for what they already have? But if we hope for what we do not yet have, we wait for it patiently" (Rom. 8:24–25).

Isn't the same true as we hope for the salvation of loved ones who don't yet know Christ? With confidence in God, we wait for what we don't yet see. Maybe it's the salvation of an older relative who's close to death. Or maybe we've prayed for years that a dear friend would come to know the Lord. Or maybe you're the parent of a wayward child, and you're praying for God to take ahold of his life or her life in a powerful way.

Tonight, thank God for what you don't yet see! Offer Him the ones you love who don't yet know Him, and thank Him in advance for their salvation.

My Prayer

DAY 2 · *Tuesday*

REPENT

Today we are considering the gift of
God's invitation to repent.

MORNING MEDITATION

Repentance. To be honest, this is the part of prayer I really don't like. It's the part where I examine my heart to notice my thoughts, my actions, and areas of my life where I am not pleasing God. And when the Spirit reveals them, I have the opportunity to seek God's forgiveness.

So there is beauty in repentance! By asking for forgiveness when I have offended God, hurt others, or harmed myself, I clear the way for Him to work more deeply and fully in my life.

Take a moment to ask God where you are not in right standing with Him. Don't rush through it. Ask Him to show you where there is a disconnect between what He wants for you and how you are living. Then sit for a few minutes to listen to Him. You'll be surprised by what He wants to say to you when you give Him a few minutes to talk.

If you are so led, share your areas of struggle on the blank page at the end of this day's prayers. Want to go a step farther? Confess your area of struggle to a friend during a visit or a phone call or even in a text or an email. Ask your friend to hold you accountable over the next seven days to consistently please God in that area of your life. Your bravery to acknowledge your sin to another might even help them do the same.

AFTERNOON REFLECTION

Search me, O God, and know my heart;
*   test me and know my anxious thoughts.*
Point out anything in me that offends you,
*   and lead me along the path of everlasting life.*
—Psalm 139:23–24 NLT

The reason sin is so destructive is that—in addition to harming us—it offends God and it also hurts others. This morning we talked about how confessing our sins to God helps *us* find freedom. Our honesty with God is the key that unlocks our ability to walk in the fullness of who we really are and who God wants us to be. And this afternoon, we're considering the ways that our sin offends God.

Sometimes the enemy can twist our thinking to make us believe that as long as no one gets hurt, anything goes. Whether it's our sexual behavior, harmful habits, or any other sinful behaviors, we want to believe that sin isn't a big deal. If we convince ourselves that no one's getting hurt, we can make excuses, justifying our sin instead of dealing with it.

But Psalm 139 reminds us that all sin offends God.

Is there a sin in your life that offends God? Ask God's Spirit to reveal it to you. Pause for a "heart check." Is your life pleasing God today?

PRAYER PROMPT

Dear God, I don't want to hurt You with my thoughts or actions. I'm sorry for _____.

Stop here and there throughout the day to check in with God. Ask Him how you can please Him, and ask His forgiveness where you have not. Repentance is not so much about finding fault as it is about finding freedom—freedom to walk in honesty with a God who loves you dearly and wants the best for you.

If it helps you, take some notes about what the Spirit is showing you. If you can, share with a friend some of the thoughts you write down. Your honesty with God, whether or not you share with a friend, allows you to talk to Him with a clear conscience, knowing that you have acknowledged your areas of weakness and sought His help.

EVENING INSPIRATION

This morning we looked at how we find freedom when we confess our sins. And this afternoon we considered the ways our sin offends God. This evening, ask God to help you notice the ways your sin hurts others.

- Does your temper hurt the people with whom you do life?
- Does your addiction or habit waste time, money, or energy that could bless others?
- Does your behavior toward others set a poor example for those who are watching your life?
- How else does your sin affect others? Ask God to show you.

Here's the good news: God's mercy is bigger than any of your mistakes. It's not too late to talk to God and clear the air. You'll be glad you did.

And what if today wasn't a good day? What if you know you have blown it in some way?

Well, guess what? He knew you would need His help. That's exactly why He came.

> "It is not the healthy who need a doctor, but the sick. I have not come to call the righteous, but sinners to repentance."
> —*Luke 5:31–32*

Don't be ashamed to tell Him that you need Him. He's listening.

Do you need Jesus today? Tell Him so.

If today was a day of victory for you, tell Him that too.

My Prayer

ASK

*Today we are expressing our confidence that
God sees and hears us when we pray.*

MORNING MEDITATION

This is the day that you have been waiting for, right? The day you
get to present your *requests* to God! So don't be shy: talk to God
about all of it. Often. As soon as a need, a concern, a decision,
an emotion, or a hard circumstance arises, let it remind you to
chat with Him. You are not bothering Him. He likes to hear
from you.

This morning, what request are you champing at the bit to ask
of God? No need to fake the funk and request what you *ought* to
pray for. Think of something you really *want* to pray for. He knows
your heart anyway, right?

This morning, pray for the desires of your heart.

Start today by being honest. What do you desire most from
God for yourself?

- A home that you can own?
- Healing of a disease that's impacting your health?
- A partner with whom to share your life?
- A job that will allow you to provide for your family?

Share your big heart's desire on the blank page at the end of this day's prayers. Doing so creates a great opportunity for a heart check in the future. When you return to this book during a new season of life, you will see whether the desire of your heart has remained steadfast or if it has changed.

Pick at least one thing—the thing your heart burns for—and go for it.

Pause. Be still. Lay it at Jesus' feet and just ask.

Know that when you pray, God hears more than you say, answers more than you ask, and gives more than you imagine in His time and in His way.

AFTERNOON REFLECTION

This morning you let it all hang out by asking God for what you most want. God loves it when you trust Him with what's in your heart. This afternoon, ask God for what you *need*.

Often there will be overlap between what you want and what you need. If you need a safe place to live, owning your own home might be a want but not a need. If you have a car that gets you to work, a new model SUV might be a want and not a need. But if you're unemployed, securing a job that you love is both a want and a need. And if you're battling cancer, healing is both a want and a need.

Psychologist Abraham Maslow, born at the beginning of the twentieth century, identified our basic human needs as air, water, food, shelter, sleep, clothing, and reproduction. The next tier of needs he identified were needs for personal security, employment, resources, health, and property. Next, he named relational needs: friendship, intimacy, family, and a sense of connection. There are a few higher-order needs, but these are the basics.

This afternoon, beloved, be bold in coming before the God who longs to meet your needs.

Jot down your needs and notice how God meets them.

EVENING INSPIRATION

If God answered all your prayers, would the world look different, or just your life?
—Dave Willis, pastor

Ouch.

Convicting.

It's natural to ask God for what we want and need. But God also welcomes us to pray for others!

Author Philip Yancey offers:

When I pray for another person, I am praying for God to open my eyes so that I can see that person as God does, and then enter into the stream of love that God already directs toward that person.

Isn't this such a comfort? Maybe you know exactly what a person needs from God. Great! But often we don't know exactly how to pray for another. Romans 8:26 encourages us: "The Spirit helps us in our weakness. We do not know what we ought to pray for, but the Spirit Himself intercedes for us through wordless groans." And our joining the Spirit's groans is what Yancey is describing.

> Tears are prayers too. They travel to God when we can't speak.
> —*See Psalm 56:8*

This evening, notice one person whom God has put on your heart to pray for. Who in your life most needs God's touch, God's word, God's leading? Ask God to open your eyes to see that person as God does. And then, as you pray with the power of the Spirit operating in you, join the stream of love God is already pouring out upon that person.

And here's another thought: Who or what do you *not* want to pray for? That's convicting too.

If there is a person or situation that you should pray for but don't really want to pray for, do *that* today.

Why, you ask?

Because it brings glory to God when you push past your feelings to have His heart for people, hard circumstances, and difficult challenges. When you pray for those who hurt or persecute you and show concern for circumstances that you'd rather not be a part of, you experience the heart of God. And He smiles.

My Prayer

DAY 4 · *Thursday*

YIELD

*Today we are considering what it
means to surrender to God.*

MORNING MEDITATION

I am not in control, but I am deeply loved by the one who is.
—Glenn Packiam

What does it mean to yield?

The dictionary defines *yield* as "to give way to arguments, demands, or pressure; to relinquish possession of something or to give something up; to cease to argue about."

So my question to you is, Where do you need to quit arguing with God? What do you need to simply give Him control of?

The answer doesn't have to be life altering.

I mean, sure, He could be asking you to move to Costa Rica to be a missionary, but He's probably asking you to be a faithful servant on the mission field down the hallway.

Take a moment and think of where God has been convicting you, nudging you, or speaking to you. What has been coming to your mind and your heart frequently this week? What step do you sense you need to take? Where in your life do you need to surrender to God's plan?

Surrender. That's another word for yield.

The more you surrender your life to God's will by spending time with Him and walking in obedience, the more you will also get out of the way and allow God's power to fill you and work in and through you.

So think about it.

Ask Jesus what He thinks.

Then, if you are so inclined, write about it on the blank page at the end of today's prayers.

What will you give to God this week as a result of your praise, your gratitude, your need for forgiveness, and the requests you've made of Him?

PRAYER PROMPT

Dear God, you can have _____. Help me to get out of the way.

AFTERNOON REFLECTION

We aren't called to walk in our strength;
we are called to work in His.

And think about this: how do you need to let go and follow God's leading instead of trying to orchestrate your life?

I know it's hard to let go. We like to feel that we are in charge of our lives. But I want you to know that some things end up being harder than they have to be because you insist on doing them in your own strength.

This is a lesson that I've had to learn the hard way. Yielding to God and releasing my grip makes life easier. While I'm responsible for what I do with my life, living a yielded life allows me to rest knowing that Someone else has an even greater responsibility for my life and is invested in guiding my steps.

Have you surrendered *that* area to God, the area where you've been working so hard?

Surrender doesn't mean you don't work, it just means you don't move ahead of God and what He has clearly asked you, convicted you, or empowered you to do.

His strength can take you so much farther than your will.

Each Friday of this prayer journey, the focus is on yielding or surrendering your life—in big ways and small ways—to the Father.

Do you trust Him? Answer the question truthfully. Then tell Him. Tell Him whether the answer is a resounding yes or a bit of a shameful no. He knows anyway. Be honest for the sake of authenticity with God.

Even if you don't feel like you trust Him, *do* something today to act like you do. Trust Him to take care of what you hand Him today.

What does trusting Him actually look like in your life? What would you do differently if you chose to rely on God to do the heavy lifting?

Breathe deeply. Take a chance on Him. What's your first step if you believe that He's good and that He's got everything under control?

It's okay if your heart is beating a little faster.

Feet don't have to follow feelings, but they should always follow the Father.

EVENING INSPIRATION

Lord, I can't say it in words.
Can You please just listen through my heart?

I know you may be tempted to jump into bed. Maybe it has been a long day, a long week, or even a long year. I know you are tired.

But yesterday we discovered that the Holy Spirit can share the deepest parts of our hearts when we don't have the insight or energy to utter a single word.

Get still and talk to God from your heart. Praying from your heart works when you're praying for others and you don't know how to pray. It also works when you want to yield your entire being to God.

Tell God that you want to surrender your life to Him. And then once you run out of words, just ask Him to read between the beats of your heart and decode the message you can't put together. He will hear. He will comfort. He will answer. Consider tipping your hands up to God, palms open, to demonstrate a posture of yielding to His will and not your own.

My Prayer

_____

_____

_____

_____

_____

_____

_____

_____

_____

_____

_____

_____

_____

_____

_____

_____

_____

_____

_____

_____

FAMILY AND FRIENDS

*Today we're focusing on the needs of
others by praying for family.*

MORNING MEDITATION

A major motion picture about prayer. Your sister starring in that movie. Neither of these things is what I would call normal. Seeing my sister, Priscilla, in *War Room* left me speechless, and you better believe I was praying for her and for the people watching her. But this got me thinking. Do I pray for my sister in the normal times too?

During our prayer challenge, we're going to be praying for our families on Fridays. Just like some families and restaurants have Taco Tuesdays, Fridays are going to be Faith, Friends, and Family Fridays!

Sometimes we'll notice that we're praying for ourselves, but we've been slow to pray for others—especially those who are familiar to us, those whom we see every day and whose lives seem to be going fine.

If my sister is starring in a movie, am I praying for her? Sure. But if my sister is sitting behind the wheel taking her kids to baseball practice, am I praying for her then? Does the normal in my life converge with the normal of my lips? Because there doesn't have to be a special crisis to force us into our prayer closets and motivate us to go to war for our lives and for the lives of others.

Prayer offers to God the stuff of our everyday lives. People *are* the stuff of our everyday lives! And those two should converge regularly. This is the discipline of prayer. Your prayers, even the ones for everyday concerns and everyday people, matter.

What normal people or circumstances do you want to bring to the Most High God?

He wants to hear about your normal.

Make it a point to pray about your normal every day.

And be sure to include your family members.

AFTERNOON REFLECTION

To win the fight, you have to have the right strategy and the right resources, because victories don't come by accident.
—From *War Room*

Where does your family member need victory in his or her life? Have you been praying about it? Start praying or keep praying about it here.

Your prayers, even the normal everyday ones, matter.

In order to be victorious, you must recognize that Satan is a thief who comes to kill, steal, and destroy (John 10:10) and that he works nonstop to disable, discourage, and defeat believers every minute of every day.

You must realize that if he has a bold strategy to overpower you, you should use your fervent prayers as a bold, strategic weapon to overcome and have the victory through Christ Jesus. Be a fierce warrior by fighting for your family in prayer.

EVENING INSPIRATION

What audiences learned from *War Room* is that prayer changes things. Do you believe it?

My middle son suffered a birth injury following a difficult birth. I was as devastated as any young mother would be that her son has a physical challenge. I took my son to the altar at church every Sunday for seven Sundays in a row, begging God to heal and to make a miracle out of this son. While my boy still has residual effects of that injury, *because of the injury* he has developed a perseverant spirit, and there is nothing that he wants to do that he cannot. While all of my children give me joy, I know all of the things the doctors said my son would not be able to do, and I've seen God answer my prayers over and over again that my son would accomplish over and above what medical science expected of him.

Tonight I encourage you to be systematic in praying for your family. (That's just a fancy way of saying, "Don't leave anyone out!") A great way to do that is to mentally picture your family tree.

- Pray for your maternal and paternal grandparents, if you know them.
- Pray for your mother, your father, and any other adult who helped to raise you.
- Pray for aunts, uncles, and cousins.
- Pray for any siblings you have, and if they have spouses and kids, pray for them.
- Pray for your spouse, if you're married.
- Pray for your future spouse, if you desire to be married.
- Pray for your children, if you have them.
- Pray for your children's children, if you've got grandbabies!

If praying through your whole family tree tonight feels overwhelming, I get that. Consider asking God to lay one person on your heart this evening, and continue to pray for that person throughout the weekend. Maybe write her name someplace you'll notice it or make his picture the background on your phone. Even after the prayer journey ends, you can continue with Friends and Family Fridays by choosing one person to pray for on Fridays.

How are you feeling about the prayers you're offering to God in this prayer journey? Sometimes we can be fooled into thinking that our prayers depend on finding the right words or having more faith than other people. But those are lies of the enemy. Are you praying based on who God is and what He can do? Or are you limiting your prayers based on what you can see or what you can make happen on your own? If you are limiting your prayers, don't.

God is who He says He is.

My Prayer

SATURDAY CHALLENGE

Today we're noticing the needs of the neighbors who live near us.

MORNING MEDITATION

One day when Jesus was teaching, a smarty-pants professor asked him what was the most important commandment of all. Maybe he was sincere. Or maybe he was trying to trap Jesus. (I'd have to hear the tone of his voice to know for sure.)

Jesus' answer actually wasn't *one* thing, it was *two* things. He said, "Love the Lord your God with all your heart and with all your soul and with all your mind and with all your strength." Then he added, "The second is this: 'Love your neighbor as yourself.' There is no commandment greater than these" (Mark 12:30–31).

For Jesus, loving God and loving people couldn't be separated. And that's why we're spending Saturdays praying for *and* loving others.

Although Jesus didn't mean at all that our love should be limited to those whose homes or properties bump up against our own, that's who we're going to pray for this first Saturday of our prayer journey: the neighbors who live near us.

So close your eyes and picture the people who live on your street, in your condominium, in your apartment building and offer them to God. Write down their names in this book. Be sure to include all the members of each household near you: singles, couples, babies, children, teens, grandparents, and anyone else who lives near you.

AFTERNOON REFLECTION

This morning you noticed and prayed for all the folks who live near you. This afternoon, pray for the physical needs of these neighbors:

God, provide _____ with clean air, water, and food to eat.

God, provide _____ with adequate shelter and sleep.

God, provide _____ with clothing for their bodies.

God, provide _____ with the work they need to survive and thrive.

God, provide _____ with good physical health.

God, provide _____ with the belongings they need.

God provide _____ with transportation for school and work.

As you pray, expect that God's Spirit will remind you of your neighbors' physical needs. As you notice these needs, offer them to God and be open to ways God might use you to meet them. (Let's be clear: this doesn't mean that you're the Savior. But it may mean that you can connect a neighbor to another who drives to the same school, or that you can share clothes your kids have outgrown. Let God provide for others through you!)

As God leads, jot down the needs you're lifting up for your neighbors beside their names in this book.

EVENING INSPIRATION

Pray for your neighbors' "heart" needs:

> God, provide _____ with good emotional and mental health.
>
> God, provide _____ with healthy relationships.
>
> God, provide _____ with the partner or child or other good relationship for which they long.
>
> God, provide _____ with a relationship with you.
>
> God, provide _____ with the spiritual nurture they need to flourish.

As you pray, expect that God's Spirit will remind you of your neighbors' emotional or spiritual needs. Offer them to God and be open to ways He might use you to meet them. (Reminder: you're *not* the Savior. In case you were confused. But God may nudge you to invite a neighbor to join you at church or to share a spiritual book that's been a blessing to you.)

Beloved, this evening and throughout our prayer journey, I want to remind you that you are not alone:

> "The LORD will fight for you; you need only to be still."
>
> —*Exodus 14:14*

Do you know what that means? You can let it go and wait on God for His intervention in the lives of your neighbors. You can cease striving to fix things yourself and watch God work things out for you. You can relax and let Him fight for souls.

The more you trust Him, the easier it will be. And trust is built with time.

As God leads, jot down the needs you're lifting up for your neighbors in your prayer journal.

My Prayer

_____

_____

_____

_____

_____

_____

_____

_____

_____

_____

_____

_____

_____

_____

_____

_____

_____

_____

DAY 7 · *Sunday*

SABBATH PRAYERS

Today we're supporting the body of Christ by praying for our pastors.

MORNING MEDITATION

Yesterday, we were challenged to pray for neighbors who live near us. And on Saturdays, we'll continue to pray for others near us and those farther away.

On Sundays, we'll be praying for our spiritual community, our brothers and sisters in Christ.

Today I want you to pray for your pastor.

By pastor, I mean the primary person who feeds you spiritually. Think of the person who teaches you on Sunday morning as you sit in the pew or who ministers to your heart as you watch online or who preaches God's Word as you drive back and forth to work each day. If multiple people nourish your soul, help you draw closer to God, or teach you His Word, don't worry about covering them all today. Focus on the one who's most responsible for spiritually nurturing you in this season of your life.

Still don't know what to pray exactly? Let me offer you a way to pray for your pastor: this morning, pray for your pastor's health and well being; this afternoon, pray for your pastor's family and relationships; this evening, pray for your pastor's ministry to you and to others.

PRAYER PROMPTS

"God, I pray for the physical health of _____, my pastor." (Pause to let God lead you as you pray for your pastor's physical health.)

"God, I pray for the mental and emotional health of _____, my pastor." (Pause to let God lead you as you pray for your pastor's mental and emotional health.)

"God, I pray for the spiritual health of _____, my pastor." (Pause to let God lead you as you pray for your pastor's spiritual health.)

Every week, your pastor is pouring out into others: teaching, preaching, counseling, leading, and more. Ask God to fill your pastor with His love. Prayerfully picture an empty vessel and God filling it up with His presence, His love, His power.

Your prayers matter. Spend time this morning praying for the person who helps you grow spiritually and encourages you in faithfulness to God.

AFTERNOON REFLECTION

This afternoon you'll be praying for your pastor's ministry.

1. Preaching
   Pray that your pastor's preaching would be bold and Christ-centered. In a world that is growing antagonistic to

Christianity, pray that your pastor or spiritual leader would have the courage and tenacity to preach God's Word fully and to focus on the saving work of Jesus Christ.

2. Teaching

Pray that your pastor's teaching would be faithful to the Scriptures. Ask God to bless your pastor's study and preparation. Ask that your pastor's teaching would glorify Jesus Christ and build up the body of Christ.

3. Leadership

Pray that your pastor would lead well. Ask God to give your pastor vision for the life of the church and the growth of its people. Ask God to give your pastor wisdom for how to execute that vision. Ask God to bless your pastor with other strong healthy leaders in the body to do the work your church has been called to do.

4. Ministry to Individuals

Pray that your pastor would be faithful in ministering to those in your congregation. As you do, pray through your pastor's various weekly interactions with people: counseling, meetings, phone calls, emails, personal visits, meetings before ceremonies like marriages and baptisms, and so on.

EVENING INSPIRATION

This evening, pray for your pastor's family. Be thoughtful in how you think of your pastor's family!

• Perhaps your pastor shares life with a spouse. Pray for that precious one to be blessed and to be a blessing to your pastor.

- Maybe your pastor is parenting young children or older ones. Pray for the needs of those children, as well as wisdom and insight for your pastor.
- Your pastor may be caring for family members—siblings, parents, or others—with special challenges. Pray that your pastor will have strength to be faithful in these duties.
- If your pastor is single, pray that the Lord will meet the deep relational needs of your pastor's heart. If your pastor desires to be wed, pray for that person who has not yet been revealed.
- Ask God to cover what you don't know about your pastor's family. Maybe it's a health condition that's private. Maybe it's an addiction. Maybe it's a difficult relationship. Ask for God's Spirit to join your prayers for your pastor and your pastor's family.

Satan is real, and he has drawn a target on the backs of those who lead others toward righteousness. Pray for protection, covering, wholeness, and deep abiding love and commitment.

END OF WEEK 1

Reflection

This week we have begun to lay the groundwork for a lifetime of prayerfulness. You've started to create rhythms and habits so that you can become a person who petitions God regularly. It's important that we take a minute to reflect on the week. What has been hard for you as you have started to take regular time to pray? For some of us, the hard part is simply remembering to do it.

If you've been struggling to consistently make prayer part of your day, consider using some of the following easy reminders to help you:

- Set a timer on your phone for each of the daily prayer opportunitites described in this book. You can also use the timer on your watch the same way. When the timer goes off, you will be reminded to engage the rhythms of Morning Meditation, Afternoon Reflection, and Evening Inspiration.
- Wear a reminder. Use an article of clothing or an accessory to keep you mindful of your need and desire to talk to God. Perhaps the best reminder is a rubber band on your wrist, a bandaid on your finger, or even the word PRAY written in the palm of your hand.
- Grab some three by five cards and write down words or phrases that will remind you to talk to the Lord. Put them

in the places you will most likely be in the morning (on the bathroom mirror), afternoon (in the car), dinnertime (inside the seasoning cabinet), or evening (on your nightstand).
- Have a friend who is really good at this? Ask them to check in daily or weekly with you for accountability!

Sometimes it just takes a few simple things to help us keep our focus and not to forget what we are trying to cultivate through these twenty-eight days. Don't let bumps in the road keep you from continuing the journey!

Now that you've spent a week talking to God, take some time to reflect on your prayer journey. Select at least one of the following questions to contemplate your experience thus far. You can share your answer with God or a friend, or jot your thoughts down in a journal.

- What has kept me from remembering to pray? How can I create a simple reminder to help me?
- What part of the day am I finding most impactful? Mornings? Afternoons? Evenings? How can I use the momentum during that time to spur me on at the times it can be more difficult?
- What has God taught me this week about Himself through my prayer time? What has He taught me about myself? What has He taught me about others?
- What prayers have I seen answered this week? How can I use that as an encouragement when I feel like God isn't listening or that prayer doesn't really matter?

Week 2

DAY 8 · *Monday*

PRAISE AND THANKSGIVING

Today we are praising and thanking God for the physical gifts He's given.

MORNING MEDITATION

Guess what? You have been given another Monday! You have been given a start to a brand new week. And you get to choose the attitude with which you greet each day. Starting with a grateful heart overflowing with thanksgiving for what God has done and for who He is can change the way you see your world. When you realize that life doesn't just happen to you but that *you* get to happen to your life, you will grasp the power that your praise can have.

If you believe that you have been blessed because God has been good, express your gratitude to Him and watch that appreciation affect your outlook. Try it!

PRAYER PROMPT

Dear God, today I'm grateful for _____. I'm thankful that You _____. I adore You because You are _____.

Want more? Grab a sticky note, a notepad, or your phone and keep a running list of what you are grateful for today. Then watch gratitude make a difference in your day.

It's easy to focus on what's wrong in our lives. But not today! Take a moment to choose gratitude and focus on what is right. Today we're thanking God for meeting our physical needs, and this morning we're thanking God for keeping us physically safe.

Prayers for physical safety might sound like:

- Thank You for protecting me from physical danger.
- Thank You for providing the home in which I live.
- Thank You for those who serve in my community to keep all safe.
- Thank You for sheltering me from cold and heat.

PRAYER PROMPT
Dear God, I thank You for _____.

Write a personal prayer of gratitude in your journal or spiral notebook. Your thanksgiving will shape the way you experience today.

Even though the praise and thanksgiving prayer isn't scheduled in this book every day, you might want to make it your goal to record these "attitude of gratitude" prayers during the next twenty-one days.

AFTERNOON REFLECTION

Sometimes, you just need to stop and say thanks.

Dear God, I want to take a minute not to ask for anything from You but simply to say thank You for all I have.

This afternoon, we're thanking God for His physical provision for our bodies.

Prayers for physical safety might sound like:

- Thank You for providing the food I have eaten and will eat today.
- Thank You for the clothing You've provided for me to wear.
- Thank You for the health I've enjoyed in my body, and the things you allow me to do with it.
- Thank You for access to medical providers and treatments I need to stay well.

Today, and every day, you can use your body's needs as cues to offer gratitude to God:

When you sit to eat, thank God for being a faithful provider.
As you dress in the morning, thank God for all your body can do.
When you do something amazing—like hug a child or lift groceries or throw a Frisbee—thank God for the abilities He has given you.
When your body groans—sneezes or comes down with a flu bug or sustains an injury—thank God for access to the care you need to get well.

Thank God for meeting all your needs.

How has this prayer journey been going for you?

While it's true that starting your day with a grateful heart can set the tone for your attitude and actions throughout the day, it's not the end of the world if you forget. Pause to go back to this morning's prayer prompt and give thanks. Stop and look around you.

What are the physical blessings God has provided that you can thank Him for?

The hard part of praying without ceasing is remembering to do it throughout the day. But God is always with you. You just have to keep the conversation going. If you didn't stop this morning to talk to God, it's not too late. Even if you were rushed this morning, take a moment and give Him a little bit of time right now. You are still on the front end of your day.

EVENING INSPIRATION

Love, please be careful about giving Me leftover time. I'm here. No doubt about that. But you miss out when you speed through your time with Me.

No matter how tired you are tonight, don't skip talking to God before you go to bed. If you turned on the TV and settled in to veg out, try giving God a few minutes of your time. If you are on the verge of passing out because you are so tired, give God just five minutes before you turn in. If you forgot to talk to Him today, that has absolutely nothing to do with whether you spend a couple of minutes talking to Him tonight. Do it. Talk to Him. Put Him first. You will be the better for it. Create a gratitude list and tuck it into your Bible or your wallet, post it on your mirror or on the fridge—wherever you will see it—and whenever you need to be reminded of what's good in your life and how good your God is, pull it out. If you need more inspiration for practicing thankfulness and gratitude as a way of life, check out *One Thousand Gifts* by Ann Voskamp.

Tonight we're thanking God for providing all we need to survive and thrive.

- Maybe it's the bike you rode to work or the van that transported your children.
- Maybe it's the wood you're using to build a dog house or tree fort.
- Maybe it's the soil in your yard that grows nutritious veggies.
- Maybe it's a child's worn blankie.

Even though you may be feeling worn out at the end of the day, thank God for meeting your physical needs. Right now, in the middle of dinner dishes, in the middle of exhaustion from another day, in the middle of running errands, running kids, or running on the treadmill, give thanks!

Find something. One thing. Anything.

What went right today?

If you look closely, even on the worst of days, you will discover that God has still been good. How can you thank Him?

Don't forget to get out your gratitude journal or spiral notebook (or even the notes on your phone if all else fails).

And in addition to giving thanks, we also want to praise God simply for who He is. If you want to go a step farther, close your day by finding a praise and worship channel on Pandora or Spotify and spend a few minutes reflecting on God's goodness. You might even find that you rest better because of it.

My Prayer

REPENT

*Today we are offering God the ongoing
and chronic struggles in our lives.*

MORNING MEDITATION

Forgive me for picking back up what I've already laid at Your feet.

Surely I'm not the only one who gives God a concern and tells Him she will trust Him, but after a few hours, days, or weeks picks up that very same issue again. Believe me when I say it's never my plan. I really want to wash my hands of it and leave it with God. But as time goes on, I feel anxious. I believe that I might do a little bit better job of running my life than God does. And so that thing I swore I was leaving at Jesus' feet somehow ends up back in my hands or in my purse or hidden in the back of my closet—because I take it back!

Why does this matter? It says I don't trust Him. Total trust in and dependence on Him is what He asks me to give.

> *I never make the same mistake twice. I make it like five or six times,
> you know, just to be sure.*

Isn't this the truth? Why is it that we need to give Him the same things over and over again? Truth be told, there are lots of reasons, but none of them negate the abundance of God's mercy. If you stumble over and over, it only means you need to admit your fault to God, receive His forgiveness, and move on!

Have a bad attitude in your marriage? Take it to the Lord. Not faithful to manage your finances in a way that's pleasing to God? Take it to the Lord. Struggling to give your all at work? Take it to the Lord. Choosing selfishness instead of selflessness in your relationships? Take it to the Lord. Eating too much at lunch today . . . again? Take it to the Lord. Remember, He already knows where you struggle and where you have fallen. Fall down seven times, get up seven.

God's mercy is bigger than any of your mistakes.

AFTERNOON REFLECTION

If you are like me, you realize that when it's time to examine your heart, mind, and actions for anything that offends God, you end up identifying the same things over and over again. If it's your mouth that gets you into trouble, it's probably not your mouth every blue moon. Know what I mean? You probably find that your tongue is a stumbling block on a regular basis!

The same for a struggle to walk in purity. (I mean, can we keep it real here?) There are those who have a one-time struggle, and there are others who find themselves falling over and over again.

And then there is unforgiveness, the one thing that our own forgiveness should be based on. You may try to let something go only to realize that you are harboring pain, deep sorrow, or a grudge that you release with your mouth but not with your soul.

If you find yourself confessing the same sins to God, week after week, year after year, you're not alone.

But what does it mean to repent? I stumbled upon this quote and think it makes the meaning clear:

> Repentance is understood not as mere regret over the past but as a new vision for the future rooted in courageous commitment in the present.
>
> —Father Alexis

It's that "courageous commitment" part that trips us up. Let me ask you, what would courageous commitment look like in your life? If you went beyond regret, and maybe even shame, what changes can you make to give you a new vision for your future? Come on, friend. Be brave.

PRAYER PROMPT

Dear God, help me move beyond regret.
Give me a courageous commitment to _____.

EVENING INSPIRATION

We all want progress, but if you're on the wrong road, progress means doing an about-turn and walking back to the right road; in that case, the man who turns back soonest is the most progressive.
—C. S. Lewis, author

While I wish that I could just eliminate the sins in my life that get me tangled up most often, the fact is that I do end up confessing some of the same sins to God year after year.

How about you? Are you tired of repenting of that addiction to alcohol or food or shopping or social media or other entertainment?

Do you feel kind of weary for continuing to confess the same sins against your husband or children? Are you worn out—or do you think God is worn out—because you're not regular in the spiritual disciplines you want to be practicing?

That's okay. Don't let a long-term struggle stop you from owning up to your challenge. Talk to Him about it. He knows anyway.

What matters most is that you pay attention when God's Spirit reveals that you're heading in the wrong direction. That's half the battle. Now, what will it take for you to turn around?

Before you sleep, remember that it's okay to not be okay. We all have our struggles. God loves you for who you are, but too much to leave you that way.

Don't let this focused day of repentance leave you feeling beaten and broken down. We all have our struggles. But my dear, know that it's God's wonderful love that won't leave you comfortable in your struggle. Your conviction is a sign that He is working in you to bring about the changes that will bring Him glory and that will also bring you good! Don't focus on what you can't get right and let it bring you down. Focus on the fact that a loving God is relentlessly pursuing you even if that means making you feel uncomfortable so that you will find your way right into His arms.

My Prayer

ASK

*Today we are bravely praying big
and bold prayers to God!*

MORNING MEDITATION

What would you ask God to do in your life, or in the life of another, if you believed He would do it? What would you ask God for if you weren't afraid to take a chance on the impossible? Often I find that we pray safe prayers because we don't want to be disappointed if God doesn't answer.

If we're single and would like to be married, we may fear asking God for the desires of our hearts because we fear God might not answer.

If we're suffering from an illness or an injury or a disease, we fail to come before God boldly because we reason, "Who am I to be healed when others continue to suffer?"

If we want to see the salvation of a loved one—a child, a sibling, a parent—we may stop asking God to grab hold of our loved one because we can't imagine how God could possibly answer our prayer.

Jesus chided several people for having little faith. Check it out for yourself: Matthew 6:30; 8:26; 14:31; 16:8; 17:20.

Don't miss out on the purposes and plans that God has for you because you don't exercise faith and ask Him to intervene in your everyday life. But don't fail to experience His intervention because you are too busy praying outside of His will either.

Don't know what to pray? Need guidance on how to direct your prayers? Here are some simple thoughts to get you going:

1. Read God's Word to know His heart.
2. Train yourself to do what His Word tells you to do.
3. Seek to think and act in ways that honor God and bring Him glory.
4. Pray—talking to God often—and believe that He hears.

Okay, friend. Take a deep breath. Now, what would you dare to ask, for yourself or someone else, if you actually believed God would answer?

Pick the one thing—the thing you don't ask for because you don't think you deserve it, the thing that, in a million years, you don't believe you can have, the thing you're afraid you won't ever receive. And pray for *that*. You are worth it.

Don't just pray about what's logical and possible. Pray hard about the impossible. God will show you that nothing, nothing, nothing is impossible with Him. Ever. Period. End of story.

PRAYER PROMPT

Dear God, I ask that You would _____.

Help me to believe. Help my unbelief.

Write each of your *bold* requests in your journal.

AFTERNOON REFLECTION

To us, waiting is wasting. To God, waiting is working.

—Louie Giglio, pastor

I know what many of you were thinking after this morning's prayer prompt. "But I *have* been asking God to move in a particular way, and He hasn't answered yet! It's been forever!"

My friend, I speak to you as I speak to myself. That thought is real and it can be frustrating, but that's not the most important thing. The important thing is whether you choose, *as you wait,* to still trust Him, love Him, believe in Him, wait for Him, serve Him, honor Him, and glorify Him every day that you get to live on this earth.

Will you be bold enough to ask *and* fearless enough to wait and to keep asking, if necessary? At the end of the day, our desires should never eclipse our determination to grow more in love with the Man who gave His life for us. If you get tired of waiting, remember this: He is always your answer. Any other desire you have should only point you back to Him. So pray boldly and without fear, but enjoy the waiting room, because it simply gives you more time to focus on your relationship with Him.

We are in the second half of the day. The Word says that in this world you *will* have trouble (John 16:33). I bet at this time of day, someone is finding that to be true! But we also see that David, a man after God's own heart, didn't just *have* trouble, he took his difficulties to the Lord in prayer.

> I took my troubles to the LORD;
> I cried out to him, and he answered my prayer.
> —*Psalm 120:1 NLT*

Take a moment to tell God about your day. Do you know someone else who's having a hard time? Talk to God about them too. God has been watching. He's omniscient, remember? But He doesn't want simply to *know* about your day or the day of someone you care about. He wants to be *involved* in your day as you share your highs and lows with Him. He wants you to intervene in the life of another because you took the time to care in prayer. So pause right now and have a little chat with Him.

PRAYER PROMPT

Dear God, can we talk? Today/this week/this month/this year has been really hard for me or my family or friend because _____.

EVENING INSPIRATION

Have you prayed about it as much as you have talked about it?

We talk about what's wrong, what we want, or what we wish we could change. But the question is do we pray about it as much as we talk about it? We will call up a friend in a second, share our two cents' worth on Facebook, or even talk to ourselves under our breath! But do we have the habit of taking everything to God in prayer? Today, and for the remainder of this week, make a concerted effort to talk to God more than you talk to others about what concerns you. Be challenged to spend more time in His Word than you do on social media. Be determined to rehearse externally and internally only what God says about a matter (instead of how you feel about it). And watch Him change how you see your life and how you see the world.

As you near the end of the day, lay down the things you hold so tightly that they hurt you. If you struggle to make requests of God and then leave them there, that's okay. Your ability to release your concerns is a function of the depth of your relationship with Him. Until then, write down your concerns that threaten to morph into worry. Keep writing them down until they no longer tie your head and your heart into knots.

Lay down tonight, knowing that you have done your part to make your request known. Now trust God to do His.

And when you offer your prayers to God in the quiet place, where it's only the two of you, don't be afraid to pray those big bold prayers.

My Prayer

DAY 11 · *Thursday*

YIELD

Today we are yielding to God through obedience.

MORNING MEDITATION

If it stops you from getting closer to God,
then it needs to go.

This morning your prayer challenge is to KISS: keep it simple, sister. Don't think too hard. What does God want from you today? Don't get overwhelmed with what He wants from you for the rest of your life. Focus on what He wants from you *today*. What will you choose to surrender to Him because you love Him?

Prayer is important. But if you squirmed a bit when you read this, good! He's speaking to you! The question is whether you will respond to His voice. You may say you want God to speak, but are you listening for His voice or acting on what He says? This is it, my friend. This is how you grow in your confidence to hear Him. You sense a stirring in your heart or a whisper to your soul and *you obey*. Then the next time you obey, you recognize His voice and know that it is Him who speaks. Do you want to hear God speak in your life more and more? Well, this is it! Today is your day. Yield. Obey. Surrender.

Dear God, I hear You telling me to _____. I sense You asking me to yield/surrender/obey in the area of _____. Today I choose to obey.

What will you do as an act of obedience today? God is intently listening for your answer.

AFTERNOON REFLECTION

Sometimes, my love, you must stop trying,
quit thinking, cease wrestling, and simply obey.

Alrighty, lovely, you are about halfway through your day. Have you obeyed? Have you surrendered? In what way have you been willing to yield to your Father in heaven?

Maybe your obedience to God today will be as simple as starting up a conversation with a colleague or a fellow student who seems like they could use a friend.

Or maybe it will be more difficult. Maybe God has been asking you to reach out in love to that family member who always seems to work your last nerve. Will you pick up the phone and call?

Say yes to God.

Perhaps this day obedience will mean that you say no to chocolate cake after dinner. Or to crossing a sexual boundary that you and God agreed to. Or you say no to raising your voice or your hand to a child who can't seem to manage himself. Or maybe your obedient no will mean that you silently refrain from joining in as friends gossip about an acquaintance.

God's Spirit empowers you to say no to sin.

Here's the thing: you don't have to do all the things at once! While God wants your obedience, He also knows that becoming more like Him takes time. Instead, increase your chances of success by zeroing in on one area where God is asking you to yield. Decide where you will focus your efforts to obey. Do you know what your next steps of obedience need to be? If so, thumbs up to you! If not, ask God to show you how you can best serve Him through your glad surrender to His will.

PRAYER PROMPT

Lord, have Your way in me. I don't just want to say I love You. I want to show You.

EVENING INSPIRATION

Let God direct your steps.
—See Proverbs 3:6

I know you might be thinking, "There is *no way* I can do this every day!" Maybe God asked you to hold your tongue. Maybe God asked you to be faithful to and diligent in the tasks you must do in your home or in your job. Maybe God told you not to text/call/email that man or even "stalk" him on social media. Maybe God asked you to drink more water, eat less sugar, or skip the fast-food lane. Maybe He asked you to smile at your husband when you really wanted to roll your eyes. Maybe He asked you to write five hundred words, make a phone call, or fill out that application. Maybe He asked you to pay a bill, cut up a credit card, or give away some items from your closet. Oh, my sweet friend who really wants to make Jesus happy, all He asks you to do is obey *today!* Trust that He is good enough to renew your strength for tomorrow. Just keep your eyes on Him as you finish out this day and aim to please Him every day thereafter.

Faith in God changes everything.

Does faith in God change everything? Does it change you? Take a moment to reflect on your day and decide whether your faith changed the way you operated. Did you yield? Tell Him how you struggled. Thank Him for where you were an overcomer. Ask Him for His grace for another day.

And what if you think you have nothing to surrender? What if you are so hurt, so depressed, so lonely, so discouraged, so broken, so confused, so tired, and so empty that you think you have nothing to give? Guess what? Whatever pieces you have, He is asking you to offer them to Him today as well. He's the Master Builder who knows exactly what to do with the pieces of our lives that we think might go unnoticed, unused, or unloved.

> For whatever is born of God overcomes the world. And this
> is the victory that has overcome the world—our faith.
> —*1 John 5:4 NKJV*

My Prayer

FAMILY AND FRIENDS

Today we're focusing on the needs of
others by praying for friends.

MORNING MEDITATION

At this point in our journey, I hope you have been encouraged to pray and to pray often. I also hope that you are being open and honest in your communication with God, sharing willingly from your heart. I pray that you are choosing to believe that time spent with God in prayer matters.

It does.

So far, this book may be the reminder you need to check in with God. Or maybe you're moving reluctantly out of a place of distrust.

Either way, you're praying. And praying maybe a tad more than you did last week.

That's good.

Today we're taking our eyes off of ourselves and we're praying for friends.

Right now, immediately, in this moment before your day gets

busy and full of all the things you have to do, text a friend to ask her how you can pray for her.

Then pray for her!

If that leaves you with a warm fuzzy feeling, then text a few more people. Don't forget to pray. If you really want to bless someone, text them your prayer for them.

AFTERNOON REFLECTION

Today I pray for every friend who
secretly lives in pain.

Sometimes we know exactly what our friends are dealing with. They call us to report on a horribly awful no-good very bad day. Or they text us that they just won a hundred dollars in a contest at work. Or they stop by our house after the kids are in bed to cry on our shoulder.

But sometimes we don't know what's going on with our friends. Maybe they're too ashamed to tell us. Maybe they don't yet have the words to express what's going on inside of them. Maybe they're afraid we'll judge them. Or maybe they just feel stuck and can't get words out.

Today, pray for the needs that you might not even know about.

Lord, help me to see what You see in the hearts and lives of my friends. Continue to prompt me, to quicken my heart to pray for those friends who really need prayer.

Give me a high level of sensitivity to those who are hurting and who need a touch from You.

You died for me, Jesus. And You died for them. Help me never to forget to love others like You love me.

EVENING INSPIRATION

Remember that you can pray anytime, anywhere. Washing dishes, digging ditches, working in the office, in the shop, on the athletic field, even in prison—you can pray and know God hears!
—Billy Graham, evangelist

Is there a friend about whom you have concerns? Pray for her or him right now. No matter where you are.

God is never blind to your tears, never deaf to your prayers, and never silent to your pains. When you are lifting your friends up before Him, He sees, He hears, and He will deliver.

Wherever you are, right this very second, God sees your friend, and He cares.

Take a second to tell Him that you appreciate His holding your friend in His tender embrace.

Then if you have a few minutes, talk to Him about what concerns you about this friend. Simply invite Him into those worries and feelings. He already knows. He is the one who knows what to do.

PRAYER PROMPT

Dear God, I know You see my friend and You see me.
I can't fix this, but I invite You into this with me.

Beloved, your prayers matter.

And one of the best things you may ever tell a friend is, "I'm praying for you."

If you can't get someone off your mind, pray for them. You may be the only one who cares enough to do so.

Have you had someone on your mind? Have you thought about them or maybe even prayed for them? Why don't you go old school and pick up the phone and call them to let them hear your voice? Tell them you care about them, that you've been thinking about them, and that you've whispered their name to Jesus today.

My Prayer

SATURDAY CHALLENGE

Today we're praying for the needs of our communities.

Today you will go to work, run errands, take your kids to extra-curricular activities, shop for groceries, clean your house, pay some bills, go to the beauty shop, attend a Zumba class, clean out your purse, fill up your car with gas, order a pizza, fill your filtered-water containers, meet friends for dinner, study for a test, move your college kids back to school, and any number of other things. As you do these things, think about who you are coming into contact with and how you can pray for them.

MORNING MEDITATION

Last week we prayed for our neighbors who live near us. This week, we'll expand our prayers for others by praying for people in our community.

Think about where you live, work, and play. Think about your community, those who lead, work, and live in it.

1. Pray for leaders in your community.

    Who are the decision-makers where you live? They need your prayers. Pray for the mayor, the city council, the school board, the superintendent, and principals. Pray for those who govern.

    Also, pray for those who are employed as servants who help your community flourish. Pray for the librarian who is so helpful when you check out books for your kids. Pray for the servants like police officers, firefighters, and EMTs who help those in need. Pray for the city workers who fix roads, collect garbage, and beautify parks. Pray for all those who serve.

2. Pray for your schools.

    Pray for the principals of the schools near you. Pray for the teachers who pour into the hearts and minds of children. Pray for the counselors, nurses, cafeteria workers, and other staff people. Pray for leaders of your parent-teacher association and other parents who serve in the classroom. Pray for the children! Ask God to lead you as you pray for the hearts, minds, and bodies of children in schools near you.

    Because education looks different for various families in your community, remember to pray for public schools, private schools, other schools such as magnet or charter schools, and families who homeschool.

3. Pray for those who work in your community.

    Pray for the people whose lives intersect your own because they work in your community. Pray for the young lady who rings up your groceries at the store. Pray for the nurse's aid who bathes your grandparent in a nursing home. Pray for the mechanic who changes the oil in your car. Pray for the high school student who hands you popcorn at the movie theater.

4. Pray for those who serve in your community.

Pray for organizations that serve by meeting needs in your community. Pray for those serving at the food pantry that feeds those in need. Pray for those working and volunteering at the homeless shelter. Pray for programs nurturing children through recreation, education, and mentoring.

5. Pray for the vulnerable people in your community.

Pray for those in your community who face challenges. Pray for parents or grandparents who are raising children on their own. Pray for those who are unemployed. Pray for those who need safe homes. Pray for those who struggle to feed their families.

Pray for all those in your community.

Remember this: your prayers have power.

All day, look for the people for whom you can pray. Love your community by praying for your community. Who else do you notice besides those listed above?

PRAYER PROMPT

Dear God, I live/work/play here in _____.

Please bless/help/reach/protect _____.

If you want to do more, think about doing a prayer walk on the grounds of the area that needs your prayers. Walk around your neighborhood and pray for your neighbors. Walk the track at your school and pray for the students and teachers. When you drive by city hall today, park and pray for the mayor. Remember, your prayers matter.

AFTERNOON REFLECTION

God has not given us a spirit of fear,
but of power and of love and of a sound mind.
—2 Timothy 1:7 NKJV

Come on, tell the truth. Does it weird you out to think about getting out of your car at city hall, standing there and closing your eyes while you pray for those who make decisions? Does it make you a little nervous to think about doing a prayer walk around your neighborhood, especially if you are talking to God aloud?

It's a Saturday. It is likely the main day of the week that you are out and about. What do you see? And when you see it—from your seat by the soccer field or on a bench at the park or in the parking lot at the mall—how will you respond?

What about actually doing something? Have you ever been moved to gather a group of moms from your school to pray for the teachers and the administrators? Or maybe you pass the fire station every day and have never said thank you to the firefighters, much less prayed for them.

My friend, God has not given you a spirit of fear. Think about how bold your prayers and your service can be when you are not afraid of what people think or how they might react to your faith-filled expressions of support and love. Just a thought.

Look around. We should not be people who spend our lives in the pew. We should be people who give of our hearts in prayer, give of our time in service, and make an impact in the places where we live, work, and play. Prayer matters.

So stop. Look around. Where are you? Who can you pray for who has an impact on the way your community lives, works, plays, and functions?

And here's just a quick reminder: God loves you. He loves me. And He loves the world we live in.

EVENING INSPIRATION

Meditate on it day and night.
—Joshua 1:8

Did you have a moment to think and pray about your community today? I hope so. If you haven't, it's not too late. Just ask God to show you who to pray for, and He will.

One way to do that is to mentally review your day. Close your eyes and replay your day, from waking up, to getting out the door, to moving through the events of your day, to noticing the people you encountered, and eventually ending up in this moment, holding this book. Who, other than your family and nearby neighbors, crossed your path? Pray for each of the folks you encountered in the rhythm of your day.

And guess what? Tomorrow is Sunday, the traditional day we set aside to focus on God and to worship Him with others. Before you drift off to sleep tonight, prepare your heart to worship God. Take a moment to think about Him and meditate on His Word. If you need an idea of what to read, just open up the Bible on your phone (YouVersion app is great for this) and read Psalm 121 in *The Message* version. It's a great Psalm to pray as you prepare to retire for the evening. I'll see you tomorrow.

My Prayer

SABBATH PRAYERS

Today we're supporting the body of Christ by praying for our church.

MORNING MEDITATION

In the morning when I rise, give me Jesus.

What happens to the world if our churches don't operate like they are supposed to? What happens if we are not fulfilling the role that God intended us to fill? Slowly but steadily, the influence of God on our culture will recede, leaving a world devoid of His power and protection.

Last week we prayed for our pastors, and today we're praying for other leaders and servants in our churches. While it's true that we can have an impact in our communities as individuals, we are called to collectively come together to be the light of the world. Today let's pray for all those who lead and serve in the church (Matt. 5:14–16).

1. Pray for Those Who Lead (1 Thess. 5:25)

    Ask God for the leaders in your church to model a commitment to Scripture and a commitment to caring for those who are outside the walls of the sanctuary. Ask God to bring to your mind the faces of those in leadership, and pray for each one as you think of them.

2. Pray for Those Who Serve (John 12:26)

Ask God to bring to mind those who serve in your church. Pray for greeters and ushers who serve on Sunday mornings. Pray for those who work with children and youth. Pray for ministry teams that are impacting your community. Pray for those who serve in the kitchen and those who clean the bathrooms! While you can pray for groups of people who serve, I encourage you to think of the individuals who serve in your church. Pray as specifically as possible.

How else can you pray for your church, the churches in your community, and the leaders in your church? What if you were a part of a group of people that is praying for God's church to be the church He intended it to be? If you don't know of a group like this in your congregation, consider assembling one if God has laid it on your heart.

Allow yourself to feel the heaviness of God's heart for His church in today's world. Talk with Him about what He wants from His church, and ask that He would move in the hearts of His people to seek His face and affect the world for His glory (2 Chron. 7:14). Don't forget that your prayers matter.

PRAYER PROMPT

God, I pray for Your church. Help us to _____.

AFTERNOON REFLECTION

We will never change the world by going to church.
We will change the world only by being the church.

Have you done it yet? Have you prayed for your church? If not, now is a good time!

What does it mean to *be* the church? We know what it means to *go* to church, but being the church is something different altogether.

In the apostle Paul's letter to the believers in Corinth—a church full of folks who are probably a lot like the folks in your church—he exhorts, "Now you are the body of Christ, and each of you is a part of it" (1 Cor. 12:27). He wants followers of Jesus to hear that each one plays a critical role. Without the gifts that each person brings—eyes that see, ears that hear, arms that serve—the body doesn't work right. For the church to be the church, we all need to participate.

Assess your thoughts on what it means to be the church. If you realize that there is a gap between what you believe and what you do, ask God to help you look like His church in your everyday as we enter a new week.

Prayer can never be in excess.

—*C. H. Spurgeon, preacher*

EVENING INSPIRATION

This evening, pray that God will continue to purify and strengthen the church.

1. Pray for Bold Commitment (1 Kings 8:61)

    Pray that your church and the churches in your community will be boldly committed to the Word of God and, at the same time, compassionate to people who need the saving love of Jesus Christ. Pray that God's people will hunger for God's truth both personally and corporately and also have hearts overflowing with concern for those who don't know it.

2. Pray for Unity (1 Cor. 1:10)

    Pray that leaders in the church will be of one accord as they lead others in looking toward the throne. It is God's will that we live and work together for His kingdom in unity.

3. Pray for Righteousness (Matt. 6:33)

    Pray that the people in your church and in your community's churches will value holiness. Pray that they will value hearts, homes, and habits that please God and will be willing to repent personally and corporately for that which offends Him.

Ask God to be at work in your church and in those people around you, so that we might *be* the body of Christ in the world today.

Were you able to draw closer to the Lord this week? Or was it a week in which your plans, activities, and responsibilities left little room for you to grow in your relationship with Him?

Tonight you have an opportunity to set the course for this coming week. What will you do differently next week than this week? How will you make room in your life for spending precious time at Jesus' feet?

Here's a heart check: is there anything in your life—any desire, dream, or even disappointment—that consumes your thoughts and actions more than He does?

It's okay to be honest. It's okay to talk to God tonight and to tell Him that He has not been first in your life, but that you want Him to be. It's not too early to ask Jesus to invade your week. Ask Him to give you a hunger and a thirst for Him, and to give you a heart committed to putting Him first and living the week focused on bringing Him glory. It's not too early to say the prayer from this song: "In the morning when I rise . . . give me Jesus. You can have this old world but give me Jesus."

Do you want a little bit more inspiration? Google "Give Me Jesus Jeremy Camp Godtube" and watch the video. It'll bless your socks off.

END OF WEEK 2

Reflection

It has been said that our prayers might not always change our circumstances, but they do change *us*. As you think back on this past week, you may have noticed that not much has changed with that hard relationship, big decision, or really difficult trial you are facing. You may be feeling a little discouraged that the things you've prayed for haven't seemed to take a turn for the better. But maybe you've missed what *is* different since you started this journey.

James, Jesus' little brother, once said, "Come near to God and he will come near to you" (James 4:8). Think about what you've experienced this past week as you've sought to draw closer to the Lord. Even if nothing changed externally, think about what you've noticed internally. Have you seen the Lord draw closer as you have approached Him more regularly?

Take a minute to reflect on your countenance. What is your inner posture toward the people and situations you are facing? Have you found yourself with more compassion for that person who normally drives you a little crazy? Have you been more at peace in spite of all the chaos in your life? Have you felt God's invisible hand holding yours as you've stood face to face with your fears?

Grab a sheet of paper and write some victories you've seen. While they might not take the form of prayers being answered the way you want, they are just as important. Write down some changes you've seen in your inner world. What shifts have you noticed in your attitudes since you've made prayer a priority? Use your discoveries to encourage yourself when you feel like you're not getting the answers you want as quickly as you'd like to receive them.

As we get ready to start a new week, ask yourself the following questions:

- What changes have I seen that are more about my inner life than my outer circumstances?
- How have my prayers made a difference in how I think? How have they changed the way I feel or the way I respond to others?
- What can I do to grow in the consistency of my prayer time? Do I need some additional reminders or accountability?
- What have I learned about God's character this week? What has He taught me about myself? What has He taught me about others?
- How can I continue to grow in trusting the Lord regardless of how He answers my prayers?

Week 3

DAY 15 · *Monday*

PRAISE AND THANKSGIVING

*Today we are praising and thanking God
for the relationships in our lives.*

MORNING MEDITATION

*Gratitude can transform common days into thanks-
givings, turn routine jobs into joy, and change
ordinary opportunities into blessings.*
—William Arthur Ward, writer

It's day 15 of our prayer journey. You still with me? If you've fallen off, no biggie—get up and get back with the program!

On the first day of this prayer journey, we thanked God for His spiritual blessings. And last week we thanked God for the blessings we've received. Today, we're thanking God for the social blessings we enjoy, relationships in our lives.

This morning, thank God for your family. Think especially of the adults who shaped you as a child. While this seems like it might be the easiest, most obvious, no-brainer prayer of the journey, for many it's a tricky prayer to pray. That's because all of us come from families that have been impacted by the power of sin and death.

No one had a perfect mom. No one had a perfect dad. (Well . . .
Jesus . . .) For example, I came from a really strong healthy family,
but of course we're not perfect! We struggle. We sin. We fail. And
in the midst of our brokenness, God is still God. And God is at
work in each of our lives.

I want to invite you to offer a twofold prayer of gratitude for
your family today.

First, thank God for the gifts you received from your family.
Maybe your dad sang you lullabies at night. Maybe your grandma
taught you how to pray. Maybe you had an older sibling who protected
you. Maybe your mom made sure you had a healthy lunch every day.
Thank God for the goodness you received from your family.

Second, thank God for the challenges you faced in your family. (Say what?!) I know, right? It's counterintuitive! But do take
a moment to notice the challenges you faced in your home growing up, and then thank God for being present with you in every
moment. If you notice strong feelings of sadness, fear, or anger,
offer those to God and jot them down in your prayer journal so that
you can continue to process them. (If they feel overwhelming, get
help from a pastor or counselor.)

Beloved, God has been at work in your life *since your birth*
through your family. Thank Him for the good and release to him
what has been difficult.

AFTERNOON REFLECTION

Afternoon prayer is a fun one today!

This afternoon you get to thank God for the good gift of
relationships He has given you with those outside of your family.

- Thank God for that BFF you had when you were ten years old.

- Thank God for the buddy who helped you get through high school.
- If you attended college, thank God for your freshman roommate!
- Thank God for the ride-or-die girlfriend you know you can count on when life gets rough.
- Thank God for the staff person at work who makes your days brighter.
- Thank God for the barista at the Starbucks drive-thru who's got your back every morning.

Really have fun with this prayer this afternoon. Let the Spirit remind you of that girl you shared a bunk bed with at summer camp twenty years ago or the sister-in-law you went camping with last weekend. Thank God for the friends, peers, and colleagues in your life.

EVENING INSPIRATION

How are you coming on your gratitude list? Did you forget about it? Grab your journal and find a piece of paper, quick! Start a new note on your phone, or if all else fails, write one or two things you are grateful for on the palm of your hand. Mondays are about thanking God for what He's done and who He is. Your assignment is to walk through your day looking for what's good, right, and better than it otherwise could have been. Choose joy. Pause right now to thank God for something, anything, because when you do, your choice will change you.

Tonight, I'm inviting you to pray for the people in your life who have shaped who you are today. For this prayer, I welcome you to mentally journey through your life and notice the folks who impacted your life for good.

- If your birth was precarious, thank God for the doctor in that delivery room.
- If you attended vacation Bible school, thank God for the adults who poured into your spirit.
- If you thrived as a Girl Scout, thank God for your troop leader.
- If you had a grandparent or another adult who was a rock for you during a difficult childhood, thank God for that person.
- If you attended youth group, thank God for those who cared for you.
- If there is one particular person who led you to Christ, thank God for that person.
- If there was a teacher or coach who affirmed your potential, thank God for that person.
- If there was a mentor who invested time, energy, and love into your life, thank God for that person.
- If there was a boss or colleague who helped you get to the next level, thank God for him or her.

Prayerfully walk through each year of your life, asking God to show you the people who shaped the woman you are today. Thank God for each one.

My Prayer

DAY 16 · *Tuesday*

REPENT

Today we are remembering God's faithfulness when we repent.

MORNING MEDITATION

Do you remember when you were a kid ever trying to hide your sin or mistake from your parents? If you stole gum from a grocery store, you might have sneaked out to the garage to chew it in secret. If you broke a flower vase, you might have hidden the pieces in the trash can. When we feel guilty or ashamed, our impulse is to hide.

If that sounds familiar it's because . . . Adam and Eve! After their sin, they hid from God in the garden. And we kinda know how that one turned out: God *found* them. Their sin was not hidden.

Even as adults, we might think we're pulling a fast one on God. If we push our sin out of our minds and refuse to confess to God, we might believe that—like chewing the gum in the garage—our sin won't be found out.

You see where this is heading, don't you? Whether you avoid your sin or not, God sees. God hears. God knows.

> You, God, know my folly;
>   my guilt is not hidden from you.
>
> —*Psalm 69:5*

Don't pretend with God. He already knows. Just be honest about where you're struggling. Rest in His love. Learn to walk in His strength.

PRAYER PROMPT

Dear God, I know that this sin, _____,
is not hidden from You. Forgive me.

If you've met God, I probably don't need to convince you that God forgives your sin the first time you confess it. That's standard operating procedure, right? What I want you to hear is this: when you confess your sin to God, He is *always* faithful to forgive you. Always. That means God forgives the second time. And the seventh time. And the seventy-seventh time.

Beloved, God is always faithful.

AFTERNOON REFLECTION

Did you know that *repentance* is not a bad word?

Sure, it's the part of prayer many of us dislike because it turns the spotlight toward the part of our souls that we might not want to see. So many of us don't do it. We don't ask. Or we ask in a nonspecific kind of way. We want to avoid our struggles: our thought lives, the words spoken too quickly, the deeds done in the dark. A part of us knows that they all move center stage when we invite God to point a beam of light in their direction.

But that uncomfortable thing is just the first step in a process that is drawing us back to God.

Conviction of sin is God's way of inviting you to restore fellowship with Him.

Being convicted of our sin, and confessing it to God, is the first step in returning to Him. Repentance is a ticket that allows us to enter (or reenter) into a deeper level of intimacy with our heavenly Father. Your ability and ongoing opportunity to repent is a gift. Use the gift, my friend. Don't shy away from it.

Ask God to convict you, clearly and swiftly, when you offend Him so that you might clearly and swiftly repent. Repentance creates a path for full-on fellowship with the God who loves you even as you learn how to please Him more and more each day.

You know who doesn't want you to repent? The enemy. Satan has access to the same information we do! He knows that when we confess to God, God is always faithful to forgive, again and again (1 John 1:9).

The next time you notice those feelings of guilt or shame, you outwit the devil by pausing to offer your sin to God, who *always* forgives.

EVENING INSPIRATION

As far as the east is from the west,
    so far has he removed our transgressions from us.
—Psalm 103:12

I love the assurance that nothing we confess could make Him love us less. Isn't that powerful? If you get to be ninety years old and you're still confessing the same sin you confessed to God when you were fourteen, God still loves you. When you really screw up and suffer brutal consequences in your life and relationships, God still loves you. When you do that thing you never imagined you could do, God still loves you. *Nothing* can change God's steadfast faithful love for you.

No matter what you've done, where you've been, what you've said or how you said it, Jesus didn't die for you based on your behavioral record. He loves you because He loves you. We repent because we don't want to hurt Him. We repent because we want to remain in open, unbroken fellowship with Him. We repent and obey because we want to please Him. But He always loves us.

Rest in that knowledge as you prepare to talk with Him this evening and close out another day that He has blessed you to see.

My Prayer

ASK

*Today we are praying for ourselves with
the confidence that God is listening.*

MORNING MEDITATION

Throughout these twenty-eight days, one of our goals is to pray for others. Because, let's be honest, in the course of a regular day, we spend a lot of time thinking about ourselves. (I know this can't be just me!) We've prayed for our families and friends. We've prayed for our churches and communities. But today is gonna be all about you, friend.

You know why?

Because God loves you. God cares about you. The stuff you are concerned about matters to God. And to connect with God, to receive from God, you need to get with God.

The goal of this journey is for you to become addicted to your time with Jesus. There are a lot of things you could be addicted to that will kill your spirit, harm your soul, or cripple your body, but talking to Jesus because you can't imagine your life without Him—that will only give you life! And guess what I know? I know that if you have been on this journey, even a little bit here and there, you have opened the door for God to call you more clearly to time with Him. You have let Him know that you want Him.

No matter how tired you are. No matter how hurt you are. No matter how self-sufficient you are. No matter how poor you are. No matter how rich you are. No matter how smart you are. No matter how clueless you feel about the way your life has turned out thus far. When you pray, you are telling God you want Him to be involved in your life. And because that is ultimately why He created you: to see Himself glorified as you live out His will in your life. When you surrender to Him in prayer, you also invite Him to invade your story. So today, go to Him in prayer with powerful expectation that He will do just that.

PRAYER PROMPT

Dear God, I love talking to You. Will You please show up in my life and in the lives of those I care for? Today I am asking you to _____.

AFTERNOON REFLECTION

When something juicy happens in your life—an awesome first date, a promotion at work, finding a lottery ticket worth $7 million—who's the first person you want to tell? Maybe it's a girlfriend. Maybe it's a roommate or spouse. Maybe it's your mom. It's natural to take our joys, and our sorrows, to the people we know care for us. Those people are God's good gifts in our lives.

But sometimes we forget to celebrate with the one who gives all the good gifts. We get caught up in our lives and we don't pause to let God help us carry our sorrows. It's natural, so don't beat yourself up about it.

But when we don't bring all the stuff of our lives before God, we miss out on the opportunity to receive from Him.

Paul's letter to the church in Philippi reminds them to take their cares to God by praying about everything.

> Don't worry about anything; instead, pray about everything.
> —*Philippians 4:6 NLT*

He is able to do exceedingly, abundantly, all that you could ever ask or think.

God is the best listener.

You've tried everything else.

Why don't you try talking to Him?

And I also want you to hear that you don't have to use a lot of fancy words to get God's attention. Whatever's on your mind, just tell it to God like you'd tell it to your sister or neighbor.

Even if you're undone—about the death of a loved one or about someone who's in trouble or about someone vulnerable who's been harmed—you can communicate with God without any words at all (Rom. 8:26)! Know that God hears whatever is in the depths of your heart. What if your tears are all you've got? That's enough. Pray the tears, the hurt, and the pain. He can handle it.

PRAYER PROMPT

Lord, You know that I'm hurting. I don't even have the words to say how deeply I'm experiencing pain. But I will do my best. I'm feeling so hurt, but I know You want me to come to You. Please see my heart and know my thoughts. Please meet me where I am and guide my steps. Please comfort me and let me know You are here.

EVENING INSPIRATION

When we pray, a lot of us wonder whether God is listening. And even when we're convinced that God is listening, we might wonder whether God cares. And when we're convinced that God cares, we might still wonder whether God answers our prayers.

God always answers prayers.

And the cool thing is, He always says yes.

Wait, wait, that doesn't mean you should order tickets to Maui for your dream vacay if you're broke. No, it means that even when God is saying no, it's only because He is saying yes to something else, something better, something later, or something unimaginable.

That's kind of hard to wrap our minds around, isn't it?

Our job isn't to understand upfront why He says yes, no, or wait. Our job is to pray and, by doing so, to access whatever yes He thinks is best.

Have you been waiting for a long time for God to answer your prayer? If He hasn't answered, keep praying. If you prayed and He said no, believe that He's still good. If He said yes, share your testimony so that others are encouraged.

My Prayer

YIELD

*Today we are considering what
we should surrender to God.*

MORNING MEDITATION

Me: It ain't much but it's all I got.
God: It's all I ever wanted.

Today is day 18 of our prayer journey. If you have found yourself praying just a little more than normal, great! Even if you are still working on consistency, that's okay. I bet you are a little more conscious about your prayer life, and that's the whole point. The goal is for you to know that God is just a prayer away, and He wants us to engage in an ongoing conversation with Him.

But here's the question. *Why* do you think He wants us to talk to Him regularly? There could be a lot of answers to that question, but here's one that I think matters most. He wants us to be aware in every second of every day how *He* wants us to talk, walk, move, operate, feel, react, work, play, mother, take risks, give, and so on. He wants us to know what He wants so we can be more like Him.

Prayer opens the door for us to empty ourselves of anything that's not like Him and make room for Him to fill us up. And why should you care about that? Well, my friend, His glory always brings us the greatest good. If you have no other prayer to pray today, feel free to borrow this one.

PRAYER PROMPT

Lord, empty me of me so I can be filled with You.

On Thursdays, as we yield to God, we commit ourselves to surrender to Him. Does that word make you nervous or uncomfortable? If so, it's ultimately because you don't trust God to do a better job with the pieces of your life than you can.

Surrender is hard if you have been doing okay by yourself. You may think that if you surrender to Him, He may ask you to move in a different direction and not give you the desires of your heart.

Surrender can be scary, but it's the only way to move with God into the life He has for us. This morning I want you to talk to God about surrendering the relationships in your life. Some of these are very brave prayers to pray, because true surrender means that your life might change.

What if He tells you the guy you've been dating is not the one He wants you to marry?

What if He asks you to keep your lips zipped about your husband's bad habit? Or asks you to speak up?

What if He asks you not to interfere in your adult child's life, because He's got it?

What if He wants you to cut ties with a toxic friend?

I know. It's uncomfortable, isn't it?

But maybe there's a guy you'll meet next summer who's exactly the man God has chosen for you.

Maybe your restraint is what will finally allow your husband to own his problem.

Maybe God is at work in the heart of your child in ways you can't yet see.

Maybe pausing or ending a codependent relationship is what your friend needs in order to get help and be well.

PRAYER PROMPT

Dear God, You can have _____. I trust that You can do a better job with this person than I can.

AFTERNOON REFLECTION

Lord, empty me of me so I can be filled with You.

This afternoon we're praying about the work God has created you to do. For some, work will mean growing in the career path that God has designed them for. For others, work might mean the job they show up to Monday through Friday that pays the bills. Some have been called to the work of raising children or caring for parents or others with special needs. And others have been called to use the hours God has given them serving others as a volunteer or as an amazing neighbor.

If you don't like the stuff that fills your days, you're probably psyched to surrender your work to God. And if you adore what you get to do every day, you might be more hesitant to submit it to God.

After all, what if He tells you that the career you think you love is not the one He wants you to have?

What if He asks you to quit your job without having another one lined up?

What if God wants you to wait before having another child, for reasons that aren't at all clear to you?

Or what if God is calling you to serve in your church in a role that makes you feel a little uncomfortable?

And what if God gets totally crazy and asks you and your family to move to another part of the country just because He said so? What if He knows that there are places to see and experiences to be had in another location and that new people and places would absolutely give you the thrill of your life, but you are too limited in your thinking to contemplate the unknown?

I know you might feel terrified right now, but hear me loud and clear on this important point.

You can trust God.

PRAYER PROMPT

Dear God, I offer to you the work that fills my days: _____.

The reason why many are still troubled, still seeking, still making little forward progress is because they haven't yet come to the end of themselves. We're still trying to give orders, and interfering with God's work within us.

—A. W. Tozer, pastor

God's plans for your life far exceed the circumstances of your day.

—Louie Giglio, pastor

EVENING INSPIRATION

I have made you and I will carry you;
I will sustain you and I will rescue you.
—Isaiah 46:4

This evening we will pray about the habits in our lives. Maybe you've established a rhythm of prayer and spiritual disciplines. Awesome! Lay that before God with open hands and listen for His guidance. Maybe there's an addictive tendency in your life—for food, for spending, for alcohol—that you need to offer to God.

It's hard to give up control.

After all, what if He tells you that your habits are not pleasing to Him and He wants you to stop indulging?

What if He asks you to stop spending so much money on yourself and commit more of your finances to things that bless others and further His kingdom?

What if your habits are limiting your best life?

If some of your habits are old and hard and ingrained, it may feel scary to let them go.

Do you trust Him? Will you surrender?

The evidence of our lack of surrender is often seen in our cycle of prayer, emotions, and actions. We pray. Then we get up and don't act like we believe God is handling what we laid at His feet.

What I want you to hear is that even though it feels scary to surrender, God is trustworthy. When you yield, God is faithful to give you what you need to obey and remain faithful.

> *We lie to God in prayer if we don't rely on Him afterward.*
> *—Robert Leighton, preacher*

Do you trust God? Do you believe He is who He says He is and that He can do what He says He can do? (Thanks, Beth Moore, for that line.) Then do everything in your power to pray, praise, thank, repent, and ask. Then get up off of your knees and leave it there.

After you've prayed about it, do what God is asking you to do. Participate with Him in living the life He has asked you to live by surrendering wholly and completely to Him. Everything else? Stop. Just stop.

Tonight before you go to sleep, contemplate this: Have you been lying to God? Do you pray like you trust Him, but then act like you don't? Just a little food for your evening thoughts. Remember, He is full of forgiveness and mercy when we confess and seek freedom.

My Prayer

DAY 19 · *Friday*

FAMILY AND FRIENDS

Today we're focusing on the needs of others by praying for those beyond family and friends.

MORNING MEDITATION

Beware in your prayers, above everything else, of limiting God, not only by unbelief, but by fancying that you know what He can do.
—Andrew Murray, writer, teacher, pastor

Happy Friday!

On our first Friday, we prayed for our families. And last week we prayed for our friends. Today we're going to pray for other individuals God has placed in our lives.

This morning I'd like to invite you to pray for someone in your life—outside of family and close friends—who gives you trouble.

Maybe it's a colleague who makes your life difficult. Maybe it's the person your sister is dating, about whom you have big concerns. Maybe it's a neighbor who seems to complain about everything. Maybe it's a committee at your child's school that's refusing the services your child needs. Who comes to mind when I invite you to pray for someone who gives you trouble?

Beloved, whoever this individual is and whatever the conflict is between you, God is bigger. Pray like God is actually God. He can do big things. Pray, keeping in mind what will bring Him glory, and ask for the impossible. God can do the impossible. Prayer extends an invitation for God to invade the circumstances of your everyday. Pray big. Then wait. Watch. Be ready.

God is good. When in doubt, just say that to yourself a few times and choose to think about what *is* right in your world. God can do all things, and He does them well. Take a moment today to think about a time when God has answered your prayers. If you can't think of a time like that, text two or three people who love God and ask them for testimonies of answered prayer. Whether the prayer and answer were your own or belonged to a family member or friend, remembering answered prayers is encouraging. Believe that God is good and that He can answer prayer. This will give you boldness as you go to Him with your requests.

No matter what may be going wrong, out of your control, or totally freaking you out, He can do the impossible.

PRAYER PROMPT

Dear Lord, I offer to You this person in my life who gives me trouble.

AFTERNOON REFLECTION

Our prayers may be awkward. Our attempts may be feeble. But since the power of prayer is in the one who hears it but not in the one who says it, our prayers do make a difference.
—Max Lucado, writer and pastor

Your prayers make a difference, so keep going!

This morning you prayed for someone who causes you grief, and this afternoon I want you to pray for someone in your life, beyond family and friends, who has blessed you. It might be someone in your life now or it might be someone who blessed you during a different season.

- Maybe it was a coach who saw your potential.
- Maybe it was a Sunday school teacher or youth leader who nurtured your faith.
- Maybe it was the parent of a friend, who infused in you a passion for cooking.
- Maybe it was a teacher who affirmed your gifts.
- Maybe it was a neighbor or another adult who simply delighted in who you are.

These people who have blessed you are God's good gift to you. God has used them to shape you into the person He made you to be. Give God thanks for the person who has blessed you.

EVENING INSPIRATION

Lord, help me to listen to you in prayer as much as you listen to me. Amen.

Today, have you been able to hold in your heart and mind the person who gives you grief? Or the one who has blessed you? If not, remember them now.

And this evening, let's pray for a person in your world whom you may not always notice: someone who bags your groceries, fixes your car, mows your lawn, or attends school with your child.

Maybe it's a person who is financially poor.

Maybe it's a person with a disability.

Maybe it's a person whose family isn't able to love them well.

Maybe it's someone without a safe place to live.

Maybe it's someone who is vulnerable because she is very old or very young.

It may be someone you share life with, and it may be someone whose name you don't yet know. Hold this person in your heart and continue to lift him or her before God, asking God to meet every need.

As you're praying for others today, consider the impact that your prayers have had and can have in the lives of others.

Have your prayers ever made a difference in the life of someone you care about? Has someone ever prayed for you and you saw it make a difference?

If so, take a moment to write about it in your journal. It will encourage you while you pray and wait for God to answer.

How did your prayer go today?

Have you been doing a lot of talking to God today?

If you haven't, it's not too late.

But here's a challenge for you: have you stopped to listen?

As we head into this weekend, you may have a boatload of things planned to do, but have you carved out time for Him?

I mean real time. If you haven't listened yet, you are missing the best part.

This weekend, find a space and a time to get quiet and just see what He says to your heart, through His Word, in your spirit about the person He's laid on your heart who rattles your cage.

My Prayer

SATURDAY CHALLENGE

Today we're praying for the needs of our nation.

MORNING MEDITATION

Lord, pour out your spirit on this nation.
Cover the earth with your glory.
—GEB America television network

Today we are praying for our national community. Oh, my goodness, that sounds like a big job! But the Bible says, "I urge that supplications, prayers, intercessions, and thanksgivings be made for all people, for kings and all who are in high positions, that we may lead a peaceful and quiet life, godly and dignified in every way. This is good, and it is pleasing in the sight of God our Savior, who desires all people to be saved and to come to the knowledge of the truth" (1 Tim. 2:1–4 ESV).

You might be like me—overwhelmed by all that is going on in our country and wondering what you can do to make a difference. But where your personal reach may not carry you, your prayers have the power to travel. Nothing, I mean nothing, is too far removed, too big, or too distant for you to pray for. There are some who are called to lead on a local, a national, or even an international level. If that is not your role to play, then it is your role to pray for those who are called to lead.

When was the last time you prayed for our nation? Our president? Our congressmen, senators, and other public officials? It's easy to become so consumed by what you want God to do for you that you forget about His mandate to utilize your prayer muscles for the good of those who lead.

This week, what have you seen in the national news that has grieved your heart, made you sad, or even stirred up fear and concern? Pray for that.

PRAYER PROMPT

Dear God, do You see this particular concern I have about our nation? God, will You please help, rescue, comfort, deliver, rectify?

Praying for our country—and other countries—allows you to recognize how you are blessed.

Even if there are things in your life that aren't quite the way you want them to be, you still probably have much more than most people around the world do.

Think about the ways you are blessed and then think about another person or group of people and how they do not have what you might take for granted.

PRAYER PROMPT

Dear God, I am blessed because You _____.
I pray for _____, who does not have the food, shelter, safety, healthcare, peace, or rights that I enjoy.

AFTERNOON REFLECTION

"If my people, who are called by my name, will humble themselves and pray and seek my face and turn from their wicked ways, then I will hear from heaven, and I will forgive their sin and will heal their land."
—2 Chronicles 7:14

Never doubt what one prayer can do.

I know you wonder if your prayers for the country in which you live make a difference.

If you aren't careful, that nagging question of whether your talks with God have an impact will stop you from praying.

Don't dwell on that.

Think of your prayers—one at a time—and give thanks, knowing that you have the opportunity to tell God what's on your heart and He hears you.

And then trust your prayers to Him. Never doubt. And if you do, pray anyway.

I know it can be discouraging to pray for our nation and then see so much hurt, pain, moral depravity, bias against Christianity, and diminishing acknowledgment of God in a country founded on God's Word.

But what if it is the very prayers of God's people that keep it from being worse? What if your prayers, small and insignificant as they may seem, are a wall of protection that hold back a flood of consequences as our nation grieves the heart of God and threatens to initiate His hand of justice?

What if your prayers are like the prayers of Abraham for Lot, holding back destruction from the place where God has been left out and people are released to depravity of mind and soul? What if?

He hears you when you call on His name.

When hard pressed, I cried to the LORD;
he brought me into a spacious place.

—Psalm 118:5

EVENING INSPIRATION

Blessed is the nation whose God is the LORD.
—Psalm 33:12

I hope you've felt empowered today to pray for your nation. Even though it might make you feel small, your prayers move God's heart.

Today, what has been the issue facing the nation that has weighed most heavily on your heart? Continue to offer it to God when you hear about it in the news and when you notice it affecting people you know and love.

One of the issues facing our nation that concerns me is the divide across racial, cultural, and socioeconomic barriers. I know that God desires unity among His people, but even in the church we won't always see the unity we should. Whenever my heart is quickened about it—whether I'm reading with my boys, reading about it online, or hearing about it as others discuss the divide in various discussions—I offer it to God.

Pause tonight and pray for this nation to look more and more like the kingdom Jesus ushered in.

- Pray for those who govern this country in all capacities.
- Pray for peace between this nation and others.
- Pray for peace within this nation.
- Pray for those who are vulnerable in this nation, that their needs will be met.

- Pray for those who are privileged in this nation, that they will be good stewards.
- Pray for people in this nation to come to know Jesus in a transforming way.
- Pray for Christians in this nation to love and serve well.

I also want to invite you to pray for those serving in the military. There are people right now who are stationed all over the globe to protect you. Some of you may have family members who are bravely away from those they love to sacrifice their time and safety to protect others and uphold the good of this nation.

When is the last time you prayed for those who sacrifice their lives for you? Take a moment to pray for someone you know in the military, someone you know who has a relative in the service, or if you know no one, pray for God to cover and protect those you might never meet who put their lives on the line for you.

My Prayer

DAY 21 · *Sunday*

SABBATH PRAYERS

Today we're supporting the body of Christ by praying for faithful servants in the church.

MORNING MEDITATION

It's Sunday! Today's the day to pray for your spiritual community, people who share your faith. Some of those people minister to you regularly, like your pastor. Some of those people minister with you, like lay leaders in your church, elders, deacons, or the person who serves with you in the children's ministry on Sunday mornings.

But there are others. Some of those people have made it their life's work, either professionally or personally, to pour into the lives of others by nourishing their souls and helping them to grow in their relationship with God. Think about who you listen to on the radio or watch on television or whose books you read. Who has ministered to you over the airwaves, with their pens, or on YouTube?

Have you ever stopped to think that those people need your prayers as well? Pause for a moment to remember what messages have been meaningful to you during your Christian journey. Who delivered that message to you?

Have you done a certain Bible study? Have you listened to

certain podcast? Have you streamed their messages or Sunday services online? Or maybe there is someone who has encouraged you in your walk of faith by simply sharing their life with you. Is there someone you love or appreciate for helping you grow spiritually? Pray for them today.

Nothing proves that you love someone more than mentioning them in your prayers.

PRAYER PROMPT

Dear God, thank You for _____. Bless them for their obedience to You and their ministry to me. Strengthen them and encourage them to keep being a blessing to others.

AFTERNOON REFLECTION

One does not surrender a life in an instant. That which is lifelong can only be surrendered in a lifetime.
—Elisabeth Elliot, missionary

Living a surrendered life is not simple. If it were, everyone would do it! Think about someone who has a walk with God that you admire. What do they do to live a surrendered life? If you want what they have, what habits or characteristics do they have that you could adopt?

- Are they committed to studying God's Word?
- Have they developed other spiritual disciplines?
- Do they wield words wisely, like Jesus?

- Do they live out their faith by pursuing justice?
- Are they faithfully sharing Jesus with others?
- Do they serve in modest and humble ways?

What can you learn from this Christian leader that you want to emulate?

The disciples watched Jesus abide with the Father. It's okay to watch others and learn from them. A surrendered life takes a lifetime to accomplish. Don't sweat it if you are not there just yet. A surrendered life is a walk one step at a time. Just keep moving forward.

EVENING INSPIRATION

God made you to be the answer to some-
one else's prayer. Keep your eyes open.

We tend to put up on pedestals the people we admire spiritually, don't we? When we see them on the stage, listen to them on the radio, or see them on TV, we might be tempted to think they have a capacity for knowing God that we don't, or wiring that allows them to hear from Him clearly.

Let me let you in on a little secret. They don't. People who minister to you may have been to school, they may have been discipled, they may even have a spiritual heritage that you wish you had. But that's not the main thing that makes them minister to you in strength and in power. People whom God uses all have one characteristic regardless of their past, their experience, and their talents and gifts.

They are available.

When God calls, they say yes. When God asks them to do the

hard thing, they say yes. When He asks them to take a risk, they say yes. When God calls them to walk in a place where they might be alone, they say yes. And by saying yes, they end up in a position where they are ministering to you. So when God gives you direction, will you say yes? I hope so. It just might help you minister to another person or, possibly, even be an answer to their prayers.

And guess what, ya'll? There are only seven days left to go in this twenty-eight-day journey. How has your prayer life changed with regular reminders to talk to God? Have the reminders made it easier to talk to Him a little bit more or a little more consistently? I hope so. I find that the reminders to pray help me be more purposeful and frequent in my conversations with the Almighty.

As we enter our last week, I've found myself wondering: if prayer isn't really that hard, if praying without ceasing and keeping lines of communication open with God isn't any big deal, why don't we do it more? Why is it a struggle? Why is it a challenge to go to God first? One reason might be because we really don't believe that prayer works. Another reason? We figure that we'll have time to talk to God about our concerns eventually. We figure that there is not a rush to tell Him about our feelings, ask His opinion about our situation, or seek His guidance for our lives. We mean to pray about things. It's just that we don't always get around to it. But what if prayer can actually make a difference?

If we don't pray or if we delay our time to petition God about the details of our lives, we might be delaying His provision, His intervention, or His favor. Let me challenge you not to wait. Don't act as if you have time. Make it your focus and your priority to talk to God this week and to talk to Him often. Why don't you have a little chat with Him before you turn in for the evening? Don't wait till tomorrow. He's available to talk to you right now.

Reflection

I don't know about you, but whenever I try to start a new habit in my life, I am always met with some resistance. When I decide to start a new exercise regimen or healthy eating plan, I may begin with a lot of enthusiasm, but as the days go on, I start to lose excitement. Maybe it's because the results aren't coming as quickly as I'd hoped or maybe it is because I've lost sight of my *why,* but either way, week three of any new rhythm in my life can be hard.

If you find yourself losing the fire you began with, that's okay. We live in a world full of distractions competing for our attention. Each day, we have a buffet of choices for spending our time, so it's no wonder we can find ourselves off track.

John Piper once said, "One of the greatest uses of Twitter and Facebook will be to prove at the Last Day that prayerlessness was not from a lack of time."

Ouch! You can change the word Twitter or Facebook to reflect your distraction of choice, but that statement holds a lot of truth. If we find ourselves overindulging in social media, Netflix, or whatever pulls us away from time with the Lord, we can't say we don't pray because of a lack of time.

If this week it was hard for you to stay focused, it's alright. His mercies start fresh tomorrow, but don't miss the opportunity to get real with yourself and think about what pulled you away—whether in mind, body, or spirit—from praying this week. Write down a few things that distracted you the most and then brainstorm some ways to mitigate those interruptions next week. For example, if social media is your diversion of choice, consider putting a limit on social media time or keeping your phone away from you during your prayer time. If late-night binge watching is making you lose focus, put the TV remote under your Bible to remind yourself to pray before you watch a show. Get creative and do what you need to do to support yourself.

As we enter the final week of our prayer journey, consider the following:

- What role do distractions play in my time with the Lord? What are some ways I can remove things that pull my attention away from Him?
- What has God revealed to me this week about Himself? What have I learned about others? What has He taught me about myself?
- What changes have I seen in myself as I've submitted to prayer?
- How has God answered my prayers in unexpected ways?

Week 4

PRAISE AND THANKSGIVING

*Today we are committing ourselves
to choose gratitude.*

MORNING MEDITATION

What's so beautiful about Monday mornings? You get to choose. Mentally and emotionally, you have a fresh start, and you get to decide how you will embrace a new week. You get to choose how you will face a new day and how you will view the opportunities, challenges, and situations in the days ahead.

On Mondays during this prayer journey, we have thanked God for the ways He blesses us spiritually, physically, and socially. Whether we live with a grateful heart is a choice we must make daily. And it's not only an act of obedience to God, it actually forms us and shapes how we respond to everything we encounter.

Cultivating a heart of thanksgiving goes a long way in determining how you will respond to whatever comes your way. Choosing to be grateful, instead of slipping into complaints and negativity, can shape the way your mind and heart interpret your circumstances. God instructs us in His Word to give thanks not only because it's the right thing to do but because we are blessed in the process. Thanksgiving changes *us*.

When you thank God for what you have, you see how much you've been given. When you praise God for who He is and thank Him for what He's done, you magnify Him instead of your problems. You discover that, even if you have big problems, you serve an even bigger God. When you train your mind to see what's right, you are leaving less room to focus on what's wrong. A heart of gratitude and a heart of discouragement are hard pressed to occupy the same space at the same time. So let me challenge you to choose gratitude, especially in that place where you are struggling the most.

PRAYER PROMPT

Dear God, today, I choose to thank You for _____.

AFTERNOON REFLECTION

Monday has been our day to give God thanks and praise, right? Today, as we start the last week of our journey, I want to remind you how this posture of gratitude can look. Here's one of my favorite Scriptures for you to reflect on and make your own:

> Thank you! Everything in me says "Thank you!"
>   Angels listen as I sing my thanks.
> I kneel in worship facing your holy temple
>   and say it again: "Thank you!"
> Thank you for your love,

thank you for your faithfulness;
Most holy is your name,
    most holy is your Word.
The moment I called out, you stepped in;
    you made my life large with strength.

When they hear what you have to say, God,
    all earth's kings will say "Thank you."
They'll sing of what you've done:
    "How great the glory of God!"
And here's why: God, high above, sees far below;
    no matter the distance, he knows everything
      about us.

When I walk into the thick of trouble,
    keep me alive in the angry turmoil.
With one hand
    strike my foes,
With your other hand
    save me.
Finish what you started in me, God.
    Your love is eternal—don't quit on me now.

—*Psalm 138 MSG*

This is what praise sounds like!

EVENING INSPIRATION

*Rejoice always, pray continually, give thanks in all
circumstances; for this is God's will for you in Christ Jesus.*
—1 Thessalonians 5:16–18

It may have been a long day. Your kids may be driving you bananas. Maybe you forgot to think about what's for dinner and now everybody is cranky, including you. Maybe it was a rough day at work. Maybe the temperature between you and your spouse is a little too cool. Maybe your car service is going to cost you more than what you thought. Your clothes may be fitting just a tad too snugly. Your printer may have just stopped working yesterday and you have to print that important document today. Your temper may be short, your heart may feel a bit hard, and the day may have gone on a bit too long already. I know. I know. I know. Still, give thanks. Add a few things to your list. There is always something to give thanks for.

If you resist living in gratitude to God, your life will reflect that. You'll complain about what you don't have rather than appreciating what you do have. You'll notice the worst in others rather than seeing the ways they shine. You'll even miss out on the ways God uses the challenges you face to make you stronger and more like Jesus.

But if you live in gratitude to God, your life will become a beautiful reflection of the Giver. You will be able to live simply, without grasping to own more things, and be thankful. You'll enjoy the people around you. And you'll even develop vision to see the ways that a situation you'd never choose has been used by God for your good.

Gratitude can transform your life.

PRAYER PROMPT

Dear God, I thank You for _____.

I pray that even after this prayer journey ends, you will continue to cultivate gratitude.

My Prayer

_____

_____

_____

_____

_____

_____

_____

_____

_____

_____

_____

_____

_____

_____

_____

_____

_____

_____

_____

_____

DAY 23 · *Tuesday*

REPENT

Today we are obeying God's call to forgive others.

MORNING MEDITATION

Forgive!

Well, good morning to you too. Yup. It's that kind of in-your-face day. Why? Because some days you just gotta make up your mind in advance to forgive the crazy people who are gonna drive you insane when you get to work. Some days you have to decide to see your roommate with eyes of love when you really want to give her a piece of your mind for leaving the dishes dirty overnight . . . again. Some days you will have to push your way through the anger rising up within you because you are tired of struggling to make ends meet and your ex is not dependable with child-support payments.

Forgive.

Why? Because when Jesus taught the disciples how to pray in Matthew 6, He rooted our request for God to forgive us in the context of our forgiving someone else.

Whether your church says "forgive us our *trespasses* as we forgive those who trespass against us" when you pray the Lord's Prayer together or says "forgive us our *debts* as we forgive our debtors" (Matt. 6:12), receiving forgiveness and offering forgiveness are inextricably linked.

Do you really want to be forgiven by God in the measure you have forgiven others?

It may be tough to forgive, but always keep this in mind: you will never have to be nailed to a cross for the actions of your offender. But guess what? Jesus did that for you.

There is nothing, *nothing,* anyone can do to hurt you that is worse than the suffering your sin caused Jesus Christ. So decide in advance to forgive. You'll be better off for doing so.

AFTERNOON REFLECTION

Are you familiar with the old saying, "When you forgive, the person you let off the hook is you?"

A lot of us are slow to forgive because it feels like we're letting the person who harmed us off the hook. We fear that forgiveness in some way is like accepting or condoning what they did to us. The problem is that when we refuse to forgive, the person who stays stuck is us!

When you forgive, you claim your freedom.

A less helpful popular saying about forgiveness isn't biblical: forgive and forget. While it's a heartwarming sentiment, we may not forget the harm that was done to us. But we can be free of its power. Forgiveness doesn't always equal forgetting, but it does unlock the chains that threaten to keep you from moving forward.

Forgiveness is letting go of something you want to hold close because you don't want to let that person get away with hurting you. You may even be honest enough to say that you really want them to pay. Let go! Forgive. Yield to the big step that God is asking you to take not because it makes sense or feels good but because you trust Him. I know it's scary to surrender. I know it feels uncomfortable to step into the unknown, the unfamiliar, or the uninvited new place.

But if that's what God is asking you to do, then yield. Surrender. Forgive. Trust. Pray. Go. Stay. Run. Turn. Kneel. Pray. Whatever emotions stir inside you when you consider forgiving, stop to pray about them right now. Pause to talk to God about what concerns you. He already knows. He just wants to have a conversation with you about it.

Choose to forgive, my friend. And remember that over and over and over and over again, our Father in heaven is willing to forgive you; you just have to make it your business to ask.

> *God has cast our confessed sins into the depths of the sea, and He's even put a "No Fishing" sign over the spot.*
>
> *—Dwight Moody, evangelist*

EVENING INSPIRATION

Sometimes God invites us to forgive others for offenses that impacted our lives in big ways.

- Forgive the birthmother who relinquished you.
- Forgive the father who left you.
- Forgive the one who abused you.

Those are big! When we do the hard work of forgiving our offenders, we experience the healing and wholeness God intends for our lives.

But there are also smaller offenses that God wants us to forgive. Remember that roommate who always leaves dirty dishes in the sink? Or maybe there's a coworker who always calls you by the wrong name. Maybe your mother is chronically late and it drives you up a tree. Or maybe you have a child whose mouth gets the better of her. God wants us to grow in us hearts that are quick to forgive.

Develop a heart that is quick to forgive by choosing to let go of these offenses as quickly as you can. In the words of Queen Elsa in the movie *Frozen,* let it go.

Family member eat the last piece of your birthday cake? Let it go.

Child forget to clean the cat's litter box . . . again? Let it go. (I mean, after it's clean. Otherwise . . . gross.)

Sibling forget your birthday? Let it go.

Jerk cut you off in traffic? Let it go.

Develop a heart that forgives quickly by choosing to release offenses.

What is one minor offense you're clinging to today that God is inviting you to release?

My Prayer

DAY 24 · *Wednesday*

ASK

Today we are praying our requests from the Scriptures.

Sad? Pray. Overthinking? Pray. Giving up? Pray. Hurting? Pray.
Depressed? Pray. Struggling? Pray. Worried? Pray.

Sometimes you may straight up not know what to pray. Maybe it's because you haven't had a lot of practice. Maybe it's because when you pray, you pray the same thing over and over. Maybe it's because you are tired of making the same requests and tired of waiting for God to answer. Maybe it's because you have prayed before and have been disappointed that God has not answered in the way you wanted. Or maybe you don't think He has answered at all.

So let me help you out. There is nothing wrong with praying your thoughts, desires, tears, needs, and desires. But sometimes you just need to borrow someone else's words, and that's okay.

Have you ever tried praying the Scriptures? Have you ever borrowed words from God's Word and offered them back to Him? God loves His Word, and the beauty of praying His Word back to Him is twofold:

1. You don't have to be a prayer whiz and come up with new words.

2. You don't have to wonder whether you are praying within God's will for your life. His Word is His will!

If you need something to pray today, start with this.

"So do not worry, saying, 'What shall we eat?' or 'What shall we drink?' or 'What shall we wear?' For the pagans run after all these things, and your heavenly Father knows that you need them."

—*Matthew 6:31–32*

AFTERNOON REFLECTION

Remember how the two big wins of praying the Scriptures are that you don't have to come up with the words and you know that you're praying in God's will? Another benefit is that praying Scripture teaches us what we ought to be praying for all the time.

Here are some verses about what God longs to give us.

- 2 Corinthians 9:8: "And God is able to bless you abundantly, so that in all things at all times, having all that you need, you will abound in every good work." *We learn that God longs to bless us so that we can do good works.*
- 2 Peter 1:3: "His divine power has given us everything we need for a godly life through our knowledge of him who called us by his own glory and goodness." *We learn that God empowers us to live a godly life.*
- John 10:10: "The thief comes only to steal and kill and destroy; I have come that they may have life, and have it to the full." *We learn that Jesus' heart for us is abundant life.*

- Philippians 4:6: "Do not be anxious about anything, but in every situation, by prayer and petition, with thanksgiving, present your requests to God." *We learn that God longs for us to experience peace through Him.*

When we pray Scripture, we discover what God desires for us. And it turns out it's not a Mercedes, a beach house, or a yacht! God wants us to experience a life that really is life (John 10:10), and in Scripture we discover what that looks like.

EVENING INSPIRATION

There are a number of popular prayer books that coach us on how to talk to God. *My Utmost for His Highest,* by Oswald Chambers, is one. *Jesus Calling,* by Sarah Young, is another. Maybe you have a book of prayers that helps you talk to God.

Jesus had a prayer book. It wasn't bound in pink leather with decorative stitching. It wasn't spiral bound. It wasn't even a book He could tote around in His man purse. Jesus' prayers were the book of Psalms!

The psalms are rich with passages that you can read together as prayers. One of the most famous prayers in that book is Psalm 23. Pray it tonight.

> The LORD is my shepherd, I lack nothing.
>> He makes me lie down in green pastures,
> he leads me beside quiet waters,
>> he refreshes my soul.
> He guides me along the right paths
>> for his name's sake.
> Even though I walk

through the darkest valley,
I will fear no evil,
for you are with me;
your rod and your staff,
they comfort me.

You prepare a table before me
in the presence of my enemies.
You anoint my head with oil;
my cup overflows.
Surely your goodness and love will follow me
all the days of my life,
and I will dwell in the house of the LORD
forever.

If you are not sure where to start, you can start by reading these psalms for your prayer time: Psalm 16; 23; 51; 121; 139. I'm excited for you to experience the beauty of praying God's Word back to Him.

My Prayer

DAY 25 · *Thursday*

YIELD

Today we are considering how we should surrender to God.

MORNING MEDITATION

Have you faded in your quest for consistent, frequent prayer? Today's your day. Push the reset button and have a chat with Jesus. Today our prayer journey has us yielding to God, so why not use our prayer pattern to launch a conversation with God that ends with your yielding to Him!

Now, simply continue the conversation with the Father. Hold the word *yield* in your heart throughout this day as a reminder to submit to him in every moment.

AFTERNOON REFLECTION

God invites us to pray in such a way that it scares what is scared within us. If you are not praying the type of prayers that scare you, they are certainly not frightening the enemy.
—Lisa Bevere, author and teacher

Are you praying *big*? Are you asking God for the impossible? Sometimes your prayers *should* scare you.

Let me share something with you. I've been convicted recently. Convicted that I have not trusted God fully or prayed expectantly because I thought it was easier to pray small and not be disappointed than to take a chance on something big and believe that God might actually come through. God convicted me of limiting His full power in my life as a result.

Just as He is asking me, He is asking you to risk being disappointed if the potential payoff is seeing Him do great things. So what if you ask and He says no? Because remember, He is always saying yes. We just may not see the whole picture.

Yielding means taking a risk. And praying big is taking a risk.

So yield. Surrender. Let go. Read His Word and understand His revealed will in Scripture. Obey His small instructions and obey the big commands. Be one of the radical few who are willing to believe that God ultimately will not disappoint when you hope in Him.

Then put your big girl panties on, take a deep breath, dive in, and trust Him for the impossible! Have you ever believed God for the big and seen Him come through? Write about those times in your journal to remind yourself of God's faithfulness in your life.

Having the courage to pray big may leave you feeling a little limp. Because you are still afraid to believe. I know you may be afraid to surrender all the way. I know you are struggling with unbelief. I've been there. I get it.

If that's where you are, pray this prayer and know that God is great.

PRAYER PROMPT

Dear God, You are powerful. You can do the impossible. I also know that You are patient. Thank You, Lord, for being patient with me.

EVENING INSPIRATION

Great people do not do great things. God does
great things through surrendered people.
—Jennie Allen, author and teacher

Your prayer life represents your will to surrender. Your prayers say to God that you are willing to trust Him for an outcome rather than relying on yourself.

The key is to pray about *everything*. The big and the small. The special and the normal. Then get up from your prayer and act like you believe God can handle it.

I know you have big dreams. I know you have grand desires. I know you want to trust Him for the impossible.

God can do above and beyond anything you could ever ask or think. Don't give up on your prayers. And don't pick up what you surrendered to Him on your knees.

Pray surrendered. Live surrendered. Watch Him do great things!

This level of faith will push you to pray even when you don't see a sensible way out, through, or around.

This level of faith will help you realize that the point of prayer is acknowledging that you don't have the answers.

You pray because you choose to believe that He does.

And you pray because you choose to trust Him between where you are and where you want to be.

Call to Him. He will answer. And He will tell you things that you did not know.

It may not be today. It may not be tomorrow. It may not be next year. But hindsight is always 20/20, and you will see that His invisible hand was always present if you trust Him one step at a time.

Trust.
Pray.
Yield!
Then wait.
He will answer.

My Prayer

DAY 26 · *Friday*

FAMILY AND FRIENDS—AND YOUR FAITH

Today we're focusing on growing your faith in God.

MORNING MEDITATION

I pray that you've been encouraged this week to take a chance on trusting God with your desires, your dreams, and even your discouragement.

Today's prayer will be different from the previous days'. Now you are going to try putting all of the parts of prayer together at one time. I know this may be elementary for some and a big deal for others, but either way, that's okay! Since we've taken some time to slow down and focus on each prayer individually, let's put them together.

1. Spend at least five minutes in prayer. Some of you will think five minutes isn't enough to really get down and dirty with God. And others will think five minutes is an eternity. Doesn't matter. Just pray.

2. Hit all the PRAY areas: Praise and give thanks, Repent, Ask, Yield.
3. Then text a friend to let her know you prayed and encourage her to do the same. You could text her something like, "I prayed today. Have you?" This is also a great opportunity to ask your friend how you can be praying for her.

Talk to God in heaven, who loves to hear from you. Then encourage someone you care about to do the same.

AFTERNOON REFLECTION

He is a rewarder of those who diligently seek him.
—Hebrews 11:6 NKJV

Do you believe this? Do you? If you really believed this truth, how would that affect the way you pray, the amount of time you pray, and what you pray for?

How do you know that your current level of faith pleases God? What do you think it means to diligently seek Him? Do you actually do that?

Write your responses in the space provided at the end of this day or do it in your journal.

Right now. Just pause and pray. Remember the PRAY acronym and find something, anything, to talk to Him about. You should be able to find something to thank Him for, seek repentance for, request, or reaffirm your willingness to yield and surrender.

Then take a moment, if you haven't already, to pray for someone who has shared a concern or prayer request with you.

Never doubt what one prayer can do.

EVENING INSPIRATION

Prayer isn't to remind God what your problems are,
but prayer is to remind your problems who God is.

Can I share something with you? I don't just talk to God when I pray. Depending on the need, I may throw a few tantrums, shed a few tears, ask Him a bunch of questions, whine a little, and straight up tell Him that I am mad. I also decide to thank Him, think about who He is, think less about my problems, reflect on how I've hurt Him, and make some hard decisions about how to surrender various areas of my life.

That's why it always baffles me a little bit when people claim that prayer is boring. What? If it's boring, then you might not be doing it right! God cares about everything in your heart: your anger, your sadness, your questions, and even whatever it is you might be whining about. Everything in your life—every moment of your day, every worry or concern, every giggle, every victory—matters to God.

When we talk to God in prayer, it shifts our focus. It takes our eyes off of ourselves, our struggles, our inadequancy, and it places them on the one who truly has the power to change our circumstances.

On Mondays we've been hunkered down on thanking and praising God. And you know what? Focusing on what's right with Him has helped me to focus less on what's not right with *me*. There's something to prayer. It's not just about whether prayer changes my situation. It's also about how prayer changes me.

Don't worry. God is never blind to your tears. Never deaf to your prayers. And never silent to your pain. He sees. He hears. And He will deliver you.

As you continue to practice prayer—getting it right some days and slacking on others—you are strengthening the muscles of your heart as you're deepening your relationship with God.

My Prayer

SATURDAY CHALLENGE

Today we're praying for the needs of our world.

MORNING MEDITATION

On Saturdays during our prayer journey, we've prayed in expanding concentric circles for the ones God loves in our neighborhoods, communities, nation, and world. This morning, on the last Saturday of our journey, we're praying for the various peoples of the world.

Genesis 1:27 announces, "God created mankind in his own image, in the image of God he created them; male and female he created them." This radical assertion means that every individual has dignity, value, and worth because he or she reflects the holy image of God.

In the eyes of Jesus, every person matters.

While there is no end to the beautiful diversity of peoples and cultures on this planet, this morning you can close your eyes and let your imagination lead you around the globe. As you "pray through the map," offer to God people living on every continent, people of every hue, and people speaking every language.

- Africa
- Asia

- Australia
- Europe
- North America
- South America

Is there a particular nation or people God has put upon your heart? Are you passionate about a particular culture? Continue to pray for those precious ones today.

PRAYER PROMPT

Dear God, I lift up to You the people of _____.
Shower Your blessings upon them.

AFTERNOON REFLECTION

This afternoon we are praying for peace on this planet.

The prophet Isaiah announces, "[God] will judge between the nations and will settle disputes for many peoples. They will beat their swords into plowshares and their spears into pruning hooks. Nation will not take up sword against nation, nor will they train for war anymore" (Isa. 2:4). We know that God's heart is for peace between nations.

- Lord, I beg that You would reign on earth as You do in heaven. You are the ultimate judge of nations and rulers and peoples.
- Lord, I pray for those who govern the nations of this earth. Grant them wisdom and a passion for peace. Equip them to reconcile instead of make war.

- Lord, give the peoples of the world love for one another. Teach us to love those from other continents and countries and cultures. And convict our hearts to practice love for all those who are near.

If you feel inadequate for such a weighty task as praying for the planet, I get that! It's big. But thankfully, the power of your prayers doesn't depend on you. Obedience to pray depends on you, but your prayers are powerful because you pray in the name and strength and power of Jesus.

Never doubt what one prayer can do.

> When hard pressed, I cried to the LORD;
> he brought me into a spacious place.
>
> —*Psalm 118:5*

EVENING INSPIRATION

In Genesis 1:28, "God blessed [Adam and Eve] and said to them, 'Be fruitful and increase in number; fill the earth and subdue it. Rule over the fish in the sea and the birds in the sky and over every living creature that moves on the ground.'"

God commanded Adam and Eve to have dominion over the earth. And that authority required them, and requires us, to be faithful stewards of the planet. This evening, as you are led, pray for the natural world God has made.

Pray for one area of God's creation right now:

- The oceans and waters
- The land, the soil, and the earth's natural resources
- The atmosphere and the sun

- The animals that fly and walk and creep and crawl and swim
- The people!

What area of creation care has the Lord laid on your heart to continue to pray for?

Friend, we have only one day left in our prayer journey.

I hope you've been blessed.

But now, I want you to start thinking about something. While you know you can pray to God anytime or anywhere, that you should pray without ceasing, that prayer is simply open and honest communication with God, think about where and when you will pray on purpose.

Where is your place to pray? When is your time to focus on prayer and give God your undivided attention, to turn your eyes to Jesus and look full in His wonderful face?

If you don't have a place and a time, think about where and when you could. Just like any relationship that needs cultivating, you have to occasionally make time for uninterrupted, intentional face-to-face time.

So where is your place and when is your time? Don't let this journey end without a plan.

My Prayer

DAY 28 · *Sunday*

SABBATH PRAYERS

*Today we're committing ourselves
to continue in prayer.*

MORNING MEDITATION

More than a million people saw the movie *War Room* on its opening weekend. As we end our prayer journey, reflect on the prayer movement that this movie started. It sparked something deep down in the hearts and souls of those who saw it and caused people to pray, or to pray more fervently than they had in the past.

What would happen if that spark in God's people never fizzled and we took prayer seriously? What would happen if God's people understood how much we can accomplish by talking to God about our problems, desires, and concerns? Think about this for a sec. What has happened in *you* as you traveled along this journey?

Are you more conscious of the time you spend talking to God? I hope so. Now what will you do to insure that you remain conscious after you are no longer using this book for daily reminders?

If you do not create a solid practice, the motivation you found on this journey will wane. You must be committed to practicing prayer.

I love that one of my friends sets her watch to beep every hour to remind her to talk to God. What can you do to adopt a lifestyle of prayer? How can you be motivated to focus on your prayer life after today?

Ask God to show you how to stay awake and aware to your prayer life.

AFTERNOON REFLECTION

Is prayer your steering wheel or your flat tire?
—Corrie ten Boom, writer

What about you? Is prayer your steering wheel or your flat tire?

If you wait until you face disasters of life to pray, God will still hear you. But prayer holds the power to be so much more.

If you make prayer the steering wheel for your life, if you develop the discipline of prayer and regularly have open, honest communication with God, you'll put yourself in a better position.

Position for what, you ask? Well, if prayer is not just talking to God but God talking back, then you can access comfort and calm even when the rug is snatched out from under you.

When you include God in your life through listening prayer, when trouble comes, you won't wonder whether you are in His will, in fellowship with Him, or in His good graces.

It's one thing to go through a storm while in the middle of an unstable relationship. But it's a whole 'nuther thing to go through a storm in a strong relationship built over time to weather the difficulties.

When you pray, in conjunction with reading His Word and walking in obedience, you are building the boat that will carry you through good times and bad. The more effort you expend building it before you need it, the more secure you will be in the storm.

What am I saying? Pray because you should. Pray because it's best for you. Don't wait until disaster drives you to your knees to pray.

But when hard times do come:

Pray hardest when it is hardest to pray.

Most of us struggle to pray when it's hard—when what we're praying for isn't happening, when we don't think it will do any good, or when we are in so much pain that we can't take one more step, much less go to our knees.

That's when I want you to remember this journey the most. When praying is the hardest thing. When praying is the last thing you want to do.

That, my friend, is exactly when you need to pray the most.

PRAYER PROMPT

Dear God, I haven't been praying because _____ has been so hard. Help me to stop to talk to You anyway.

EVENING INSPIRATION

Before you sleep, PRAY.
When you wake up, PRAY.
When life gets hard, PRAY.
When you're happy, PRAY.
When you're unsure, PRAY.

Twenty-eight days have come and gone. But this is only the last day of our praying together, you and I, not the end of your call to pray without ceasing. Every day, you are issued a personal challenge. Every day, you are extended an invitation. You are given a daily opportunity to chat with the creator of the universe. Every minute of every day. You can pray, anytime, anywhere. Will you? Will you choose to keep showing up and having a conversation with God, being open and available when He wants to talk to you?

Because, my love, that's the secret. Showing up. Checking in. That's what praying without ceasing is all about.

Just like you check in multiple times on social media to see what you've missed, you can check in with God to talk about what's transpired in your heart since your last conversation.

Check in to see if He has any updates for you. Prayer is simply open, honest communication with God. I know sometimes the discipline might be a little difficult to maintain, but it's worth it.

The daily, ongoing challenge I'm issuing you is the same challenge that I'm issuing myself: to pray without ceasing. Why? Because that's the only way we can experience the fullness of the life He has for us. A life lived for God begins when we converse with God.

Begin that conversation each and every day.

CREATING YOUR PRAYER PLAN

Day 29 and Beyond

You made it to the end of our journey! Kudos to you for giving time and attention to your relational conversation with God. I'm sure you know that this is not the end of your conversations with the Lord. Now is the time to think about how you can continue the habits you've formed the past four weeks. I don't want to just leave you here; I want to help you figure out the best plan for keeping prayer a priority in your normal day-to-day.

First, let's think about what has hindered you the most. What are your greatest challenges to being prayerful? Is it time? Is it distraction? Is it the fact that you forget? Think about it and make a list.

Now come up with simple ways to deal with those challenges. Here are some thoughts and suggestions that might help you as you work your way through your list:

- If time is an issue, do you need to wake up just ten minutes earlier? If you find yourself distracted by your phone, can you turn it off and leave it in another room? If you find yourself forgetting, what simple tools can help you to remember?

Look back at the End of Week 1 Reflection to guide you (p. 47).

- Some other easy ideas? Grab a whiteboard at the office supply store and place it where you will see it in your home or office. Write down some of the prompts in this prayer book that you found most helpful and repeat them more frequently in the future.
- You can also grab some popsicle sticks and write things or people to pray for on each one. Stick them in a jar somewhere you frequent (like your kitchen) and pull one out every time you go by it and pray for whatever is on the stick.
- Like my sister taught us in the movie *War Room,* you can convert a closet into a place of prayer. You can be creative in this to simply remind yourself that God is there and *wants* to talk to you.

Think about how the past twenty-eight days have changed you. Make another list of what you've learned and put it up to remind you of the power and purpose of prayer. God uses our time with Him to grow us and mature our faith. He takes our conversations with Him and teaches us more and more about His faithfulness. He invites us to know Him in an even deeper way. Storming heaven's gates on behalf of others keeps us from getting stuck in the never-ending cycle of self-focus that we (ahem, I . . .) can get stuck in. Having the *why* of prayer somewhere that you can see it will keep encouraging you to stop to talk to the Lord.

Think of someone you can invite into your plan as well. Maybe you have a friend or spouse, someone you know to be a prayer warrior. Ask them to help you keep on your journey of being fervent and consistent in prayer.

Prayer is our conduit into relationship with God. Just like any relationship, our relationship with God requires time, intentionality, and consistent deposits of our hearts while listening to His. Don't let distraction or forgetfulness throw you; just pick up where you left off with Him. He is ready and willing to listen and wants to talk to you, no matter how long it has been. These past twenty-eight days were just a beginning for you and me, a push in the right direction, and now we need simply to press forward in what God wants to continue to do in and through us and our prayers.

My prayer for you?

I pray that this guide has helped you to start or restart your journey of prayer and that you will continue to enjoy the journey as you engage in wonderful conversations with a God who loves to engage in conversation with you.

PRAYER
DIRECTORY

My hope is that you have experienced the benefits of talking to God and know firsthand the value of prioritizing your time of prayer. Whether your prayer journey has resulted in answered prayers, a deeper sense of God's presence, or the release of unneeded anxiety and worry, conversation with God is a blessing to you—when you use it.

But I do understand that for many people, praying comfortably and with confidence takes time. While I believe with all of my heart that this twenty-eight-day journey will help with that, I want to provide a few prayers to get you going if you need a place to start. If you have completed the twenty-eight-day journey, I don't want to leave you stranded as you continue in your relationship with God. I want to help you grow in learning what to talk to the Lord about by giving you some prayers you can use, on any given day, for whatever you are dealing with or see others struggling with.

In this section of the book, I've gathered some simple prayers you can pray and some Scripture references you can easily look to as a source of comfort and as words to give right back to God. Write them down on Post-it notes and stick them in your car or at your desk, and use them as simple reminders that God is real and oh so very near.

PRAYER FOR JOY AND CONTENTMENT

God, I want to be satisfied—satisfied with You and satisfied with the life You've given me. I want to be a person who is overflowing with joy, and to be content with what I have while I wait for what I want. To be honest, though, many days I don't feel joy, and often I have a deep-seated discontent with my life. Would You teach me how to access the joy that You offer and to walk with contentment and satisfaction with all You've given me? Would You show me all the things in my life that I can smile at, and would You open my eyes to all that You have provided so that I can see that You have given me all I need? I don't want to be a complaining person who dwells on what's not right or on what I don't have. I want You to be the source of my joy and contentment, because You, the God of the universe, are for me, and in You I have everything I need.

SCRIPTURES TO REFLECT ON: Psalm 16:11; 34:10b; 47:1; 95:1-2; Romans 15:13; Philippians 4:11-13; Galatians 5:22-23; 1 Timothy 6:6-12; James 1:2

PRAYER FOR HARD DAYS

Dear Lord, today is a battle. Life is difficult right now. You know all the details. You know all my concerns. You know how the enemy is attacking me in this place. Lord, will You send me reminders of Your presence and love? When my soul is restless and anxious, will You give me peace? When I have no strength, will You be mine? God, sometimes I can't even form a sentence but can say only one word: help. Be so near, and even if my circumstances don't change, show me Your power to sustain me.

PRAYER FOR WISDOM

God, I have so many decisions to make, and none of them feels simple. I want to do the right thing and take steps today that I will not regret later, and I want Your help in order to come to the best conclusions possible. In the Bible, Solomon asked You for wisdom and You were pleased with his request. Your Word also says that the fear of the Lord is the beginning of wisdom, so I'm starting with You, God. Please take my desire to honor You with my life and my desire to obey Your Word and guide me into the best course of action. Let my decisions and actions bring glory to Your name and work out over time for You, my God. I trust You to lead, guide, and direct me. Give me discernment when I need it and order my steps according to Your purposes for my life.

PRAYER FOR MARRIAGE

Dear Lord, my marriage is so challenging right now. I'm tired of the arguing, the disagreements, the loneliness, and the pain. I want my marriage to be a testimony to what You can do in the life of a couple. I want You to turn our relationship into something neither I nor my spouse could have imagined. Please help me to be kind with my words and actions. Show me what You love about my spouse, and help me to love better. But also, God, can You please plant a desire in my spouse's heart to want the same thing? Can You cause us to want unity because that is what You want for us? Would You guide us individually and together to people, places, or resources that will help us to grow in our connection with each other as we grow in You? Convict me where I need to change, challenge me when I need to be still and be quiet, and keep me patient while I do what I can and then wait on You to do the rest. Hear my heart, O God.

SCRIPTURES TO REFLECT ON: Proverbs 5:18–19; 12:4; 18:22; Matthew 19:4–6; Ephesians 5:22–33; Colossians 3:18–19

PRAYER FOR SINGLENESS

Dear Lord, I know that being single can be a good thing, but right now it doesn't feel good. I want to be married and I'm tired of waiting for my turn to know love and commitment. I honestly often wonder, "Why not me?" I love You and try my best to serve You. I'm not sure that I understand why You are allowing me to remain single when my heart desires a relationship. That said, I want to continue to bring You my desire, and then to seek You for connection and to enjoy the community of believers that You have given me. Help me when I feel lonely. Guide me to new relationships and friendships that will give me opportunities to serve others and to be served by others. Teach me to be satisfied with You even while I ask You for my desires involving people I deal with in my physical world every day. Guide me as I seek to maximize the time and freedom I have and to fully engage in my season of singleness.

SCRIPTURES TO REFLECT ON: Joshua 1:5–6; Psalm 25:16; 119:9–10; 139:7–10; Song of Solomon 2:7; 3:5; 8:4; Ecclesiastes 3:1–8; Isaiah 41:10; 43:2–3; Matthew 6:33; Romans 12:1; 1 Corinthians 7:7–8; 7:34; 2 Corinthians 6:14; Titus 2:6

PRAYER FOR GRIEF

Dear Jesus, this loss is so painful. I know You understand more than anyone what it is like to feel so deeply the wounds of grief. I wish loss didn't have to be a part of life. It's so hard. The sadness is so intense and the disappointment is so heavy.

Sometimes, I honestly don't know if I can keep going. Every step is so hard and takes so much effort. Also, Lord, I have questions. I don't understand why You allowed the person I loved so much to pass away when they did or the way they did. I really need Your comfort right now. Help me to see and sense Your care for me in this valley. Teach me what You want me to learn from my ache. Surround me with people who love me and can walk with me through this. As I receive comfort from others, give me eyes to see who around me needs to receive comfort too. God, please heal my broken heart.

SCRIPTURES TO REFLECT ON: Psalm 34:18; 73:26; 147:3; Isaiah 53:4–6; Matthew 5:1–4; John 14:1; 2 Corinthians 1:3–6; Revelation 21:4

PRAYER FOR FORGIVING ANOTHER PERSON

Lord, You know how they hurt me. You heard what they said and You saw what they did. You also know how they have injured my soul. I know I'm supposed to forgive them. I know the Bible tells me to forgive, and I've heard many people talk about the freedom I will experience when I do. But I'm having a hard time doing it. The pain is still there. The anger is still present. The tears still fall. So I'm coming to You again today to be honest with You about my feelings but also to tell You that I release that person from what they did to me. I'm deciding to let them off the hook for hurting me. While my emotions may need some time to catch up and while forgiveness might not mean that my engagement or level of relationship with them stays the same, I bring to You my intention to forgive them. Help me to continue to forgive because You forgive me too. Help me to walk with a heart of forgiveness so that I can be free—free to love, free to feel, free to experience all of the joy You desire to give me. Thank You for Your help, Lord.

SCRIPTURES TO REFLECT ON: Psalm 86:5; Matthew 6:12, 14–15; Mark 11:25; Luke 6:37; 17:4; 2 Corinthians 2:5–8, 10; Ephesians 4:32; Colossians 3:13

PRAYER FOR THE DESIRE TO PRAY OR TO READ GOD'S WORD

Father, I know that being in Your Word and having an active prayer life are essential to staying connected to You. You've given me prayer for my benefit. I repent of my prayerlessness. I want to spend more time in Your Word and in communication with You. Right now, I do not have the desire to pray as I ought, so increase my desire for time with You, Lord. Help me build the fruit of self-control when my mind wanders or gets distracted. I want to honor and please You with all my heart, all my soul, all my mind, and all my strength. Thank You for meeting me here.

SCRIPTURES TO REFLECT ON: Psalm 27:4, 8; Matthew 6:6; 26:41; John 15:4; Hebrews 4:12–13; 11:6

PRAYER FOR SELF-CONTROL

Father God, help me to practice self-control over my mind, body, and spirit. Help me to make every thought captive that does not line up with the truth of Your Word. Let Your Word take root in my heart, mind, and spirit so that I may recall Your truth in all circumstances. Help me to resist the temptations of my flesh and to guard what my eyes see, what my ears hear, what my mouth says, and where my feet go. Help me to control my mouth, which often wants to speak judgment and unkind words. Your Word says that the tongue has the power of life and death. Help me to use my words to uplift, encourage, and speak truth in worship to You. With the help of Your Holy Spirit, help me to present my body as a living sacrifice that is holy and honorable. Thank You for giving me the grace to overcome the flesh and exercise self-control.

SCRIPTURES TO REFLECT ON: Proverbs 18:21; Romans 7:25; 12:1–2; 1 Corinthians 6:19–20; 10:13; Philippians 2:3–5; 4:8–9; James 1:19–21

PRAYER FOR REST

Lord, I thank You that in a busy and often hurried world, I can find rest in You. I thank You that I do not have to be weighed down by all the needs I must meet and the responsibilities I must fulfill. I can come to You, Father, and give You all my burdens, and in return You will give me rest. Help me, Father, not to wait until things become overwhelming and chaotic before entering into the rest You have promised.

SCRIPTURES TO REFLECT ON: Isaiah 40:31; Matthew 11:28-29; Hebrews 4:9-11

PRAYER FOR FRIENDSHIP

Lord, You've been the ultimate friend to me. I recognize my desire and need for lifegiving friendships. Women to lean on, women to encourage one another, women to laugh together and cry together and everything in between. I know You care for me, and I ask that You will lead me to the right friendships.

Help me, Holy Spirit, to be the kind of friend You would have me be to those around me: loving, kind, truth-telling, wise, faithful, and committed. Show me the women who need to be seen, heard, and noticed.

Help me celebrate the special people You've already placed in my life and not take them for granted. Help me serve their needs as Christ serves me, building them up in every way possible. Remind me to give grace often, forgive freely, and love deeply.

PRAYER FOR COMMUNITY

Heavenly Father, thank You for the gift of community. I recognize that I often overlook the communities I am within, but I know that You do not intend for us to exist alone. We are better together, and You intend for us stand together. Help me always to see and acknowledge Your good works in the people who form my community. Please cover and protect my community from sickness, disease, harm, danger, negativity, and divisions. Let it be a place of prosperity, kindness, and love where Your omnipresence shines through. I ask that You grow us as one and draw us collectively closer to You. Allow me to be a blessing to those around me. Help me to serve my community in a way that allows all to see You through me.

SCRIPTURES TO REFLECT ON: Proverbs 27:17; Mark 12:31; Romans 12:5, 16

PRAISE PROMPTS

When you enter His presence with praise, He enters your circumstances with power.

Praise and thanksgiving are important parts of our communication with God. Sometimes, thanksgiving feels easier than praise. Thanksgiving is all about what God has done for us, but praise has absolutely nothing to do with us. Praise is recognizing who God is and marveling at His outstanding qualities. Praise means focusing on God for His sake, not ours. But here's the blessing of non-self-centered praise: God inhabits the praises of His people (Ps. 22:3).

Our ability to praise who God is, is determined by what we know about God and what we understand about His character. I've found that many people are intimidated by the concept of praising God because they don't know what to praise Him for beyond His being good or merciful.

God is so big, and there are awesome parts of His character that we can come to know and then be able to stand in awe of Him in new ways.

The beauty of praising God is that when we engage often and consistently in this aspect of prayer, focusing on who God is *just because,* God draws near to us. Praise of God because He *is* becomes a blessing to us. When we talk to Him about how great He is, whether or not we can see the benefits, we can rest in knowing that it does benefit us when we see Him as He really is.

When we praise God, He gets bigger. And as God grows greater in our eyes, our problems get smaller. When we focus on who God is, then we see how magnificent He is compared with our problems. And He draws nigh.

Use this day to praise Him. You can either take one of the following attributes of God now and save some for later, or do them all at once. You can even make your own list of attributes. Whichever way you choose, think this: "If God never did another thing for me, I would praise Him because _____."

Use the following list of attributes to build up your prayers. I've included prayers of praise to help you develop in this area of your prayer life. Engage longer in praise without rushing to the asking part. Know that time spent praising God deepens your relationship with Him, and that as your relationship with God grows, you will also be blessed.

GOD IS OMNIPRESENT

God is present everywhere, all the time. And to top it off, He never sleeps (Ps. 121:3). Since God is a present God, we are able to be courageous. He is always there, and He is always with us (Prov. 15:3).

> Lord, thank You for being an omnipresent Father. A Father who's always here, and always there. You are here in the now, and there in my future and unknowns. You are with me in the middle of the hard stuff, and You are with me to celebrate small and big moments. Thank You for Your promise that You will never leave me or forsake me. I can count on the fact that Your presence also means that You are alert,

aware, and concerned with the things that concern me. Your presence lets me know that I am not alone no matter what the enemy says. You are Emmanuel, God with me. Thank You for being an omnipresent God (Isa. 46:9–10).

GOD IS OMNISCIENT

God is all knowing. He is aware of every moment of every day and knows exactly what we are up against. A. W. Tozer says, "God perfectly knows Himself and, being the source and author of all things, it follows that He knows all that can be known. And this He knows instantly and with a fullness of perfection that includes every possible item of knowledge concerning everything that exists or could have existed anywhere in the universe at any time in the past or that may exist in the centuries or ages yet unborn." Because God is all knowing, we can trust Him. He knows where we are, where we are going, and what we need to traverse the in-between. He knows everything. Where we go. What we think. What we do and say. His knowledge is "lofty" (Ps. 139:1–6).

Lord, I'm so glad that You know everything—especially because there is so much that I don't know. I struggle with fear at times because I wish that I had the answer to many questions about my life and that I knew the outcome of my situations. I praise You because You are God and You know everything. I'm grateful that I can rest in You because You know where I've been, where I'm going, and where I am right now. You see the problems and the solutions, the blessings and the burdens, the beginning and the end. Please help me trust You when I can't see, simply because I believe that You see all.

GOD IS OMNIPOTENT

God has all power. No matter what impossible situation or task we are facing today, nothing is too difficult for the Lord (Gen. 18:14).

> God, I'm so glad to know that nothing I face is too big or too hard. I praise You for being an all-powerful God who not only cares about me but also can do something about the things that concern me. I'm amazed at the power You exhibit by keeping the physical world in motion. I'm also amazed at the power You show by keeping my inner world intact. You brought the world into existence. You allowed me to have an existence too. Your strength and might to cause the world to be—to cause my world to be—is unmatched and unrepeatable. I'm so grateful that the God I serve has the power to do the impossible. Help me to trust in Your power when I feel powerless.

GOD IS ETERNAL

God has no beginning or end. He is not confined to time. This means He existed before we were born and will continue to exist after our time on earth ends. We can trust Him with our past and our future. He takes all things into consideration as He works all things together for our good. He sits outside of time, something you and I simply cannot do in our humanness. He lives forever (Deut. 32:40).

> Father, I praise You that there is no beginning or ending to Your existence. You stretch eternally into what was, what is, and what will come. My human mind cannot even begin to fathom Your eternal nature. I know that You hold my past,

my present, and my future fully in Your hands. Your Word says that "the eternal God is a dwelling place, and underneath are the everlasting arms" (Deut. 33:27 NASB). Let me dwell securely knowing that You hold my entire life—both here on earth and eternally—safely in Your hands. I praise You that You are not confined to time and that with You there is no beginning or ending.

GOD IS IMMUTABLE

God never changes. While many things in our lives will change, God is not one of them. Isn't that good to know (Mal. 3:6)?

Lord, this world is constantly changing. In the midst of all the uncertainties and changes that I face each and every day, I praise You that You will never change. I can rest in the fact that You are the same yesterday, today, and forever. I celebrate the immutable character of Your love and Your nature.

GOD IS INCOMPREHENSIBLE

God is beyond our understanding. He knows what He is doing. Even when His ways are not clear to us, we praise Him because they are always clear to Him (Job 11:7; Isa. 55:8–9)!

Thank You, Father, for being incomprehensible. Lord, sometimes that can feel scary, but today I choose to find peace that You know exactly what You are doing. And even though I may not understand it all, I know that all things work together for good to those who love and diligently seek You. I praise You because Your ways are not my ways and

Your thoughts are not my thoughts. Your ways and Your thoughts are perfect, and because they are perfect, they are beyond what I can comprehend. So I rest in the fact that You, the incomprehensible God, are in control and know exactly how to handle the life that I have surrendered and the lives around me.

GOD IS SELF-EXISTENT

God depends on nothing outside of Himself for His existence (Ex. 3:14).

Father God, in the beginning You were there. You were not created, and You were not formed. You have always existed and still exist. Everything that exists in this world and in me is because You exist. Without You there is nothing. You do not depend on food, water, or any other thing. You are life. You are love. And You are God. I thank You that because You *are*, I am. Because You are the source of everything and do not depend on anything, I can depend on You without worrying that You will fail. You cannot weaken or die. You are light, and You are God.

GOD IS SELF-SUFFICIENT

God does not need anything. We cannot give Him anything that is not already His (Ps. 50:12).

You are to be greatly praised. All that I have belongs to You. Everything in this world is Yours. There is nothing I can give You that You don't already have (Ps. 50:12). There is nothing that You need from me, not even _____.

How freeing it is to know that You are pleased with me because I am who You created me to be, and not because of anything I have, anything I can do, or anything I have done. You're not depending on me. It is You who lacks no good thing. You have no needs. You give me life and breath (Acts 17:24–25). Sometimes I forget, and You might have to remind me, but You alone are God. You don't need my help! I praise You, God, for Your self-sufficiency.

GOD IS INFINITE

God has no limits. Neither heaven nor earth can contain Him (1 Kings 8:27).

I praise You, Lord, that You are infinite. There are no limits to Your greatness or Your strength. There are no bounds to Your presence or Your fullness. You see beyond all that my finite self can see. Nothing in heaven or earth can contain You. Lord, You are not limited by any circumstances or by my personal limitations in understanding You. Great are You, Lord, and abundant is Your strength. Your understanding is infinite (Ps. 147:5).

GOD IS TRANSCENDENT

God is above creation and exists apart from it. His ways and thoughts are higher than ours (Isa. 55:8).

Far above and independent of creation, You exist outside of space and time. Your ways are unlike any of my ways. Your thoughts are higher than mine. I cannot fully

comprehend, but I sense Your transcendence when I'm
_____. All of creation points to Your transcendence, and yet You exist apart from it.

GOD IS SOVEREIGN

God is in control and supreme. He does whatever He pleases (Ps. 135:6).

I will praise You, O Lord, for You are King of kings, and Lord of lords. All power belongs to You. God, You are supreme, and You do whatever You please (Ps. 135:6). In moments of difficulty, when I don't understand, I find rest in knowing that You are in control. God, I praise You, for You are in control of _____. You have allowed these things for Your glory and my good (Rom. 8:28). Your plans for all things in heaven and on earth will prevail (Job 42:2).

GOD IS HOLY

God is morally excellent and perfect. He is the standard against which we measure our thoughts, actions, and heart (Ex. 15:11).

In a world where the standard of what is morally right and wrong is constantly moving, Lord, I praise You for Your perfect holiness. You are the definition of morality, goodness, justice, perfection. Your holiness is the measure by which I am to compare my thoughts, actions, and heart. There is no greater glory than Yours, O God. You are perfect in all Your ways, and I praise You for that.

GOD IS RIGHTEOUS

God always does what's right. Enough said (Deut. 32:4).

Just and true are Your ways, O God! In a world teeming with injustice and inequity, I can count on Your righteousness as my standard of living. You always do what is right for me, and I give You the glory! Thank You for calling me into a right relationship with You, that Your righteousness may be reproduced in me. "Righteousness and justice are the foundation of Your throne; lovingkindness and truth go before You" (Ps. 89:14 NASB).

BOOKS ON PRAYER

Arthur, Kay. *Lord, Teach Me to Pray in Twenty-Eight Days.*

Batterson, Mark. *The Circle Maker: Praying Circles around Your Biggest Dreams and Greatest Fears.*

Bennett, Arthur. *The Valley of Vision: A Collection of Puritan Prayers and Devotions.*

Briscoe, Jill. *Prayer That Works.*

Chambers, Oswald. *My Utmost for His Highest.*

Cymbala, Jim. *Breakthrough Prayer: The Secret of Receiving What You Need from God.*

Evans, Tony. *Kingdom Prayer: Touching Heaven to Change Earth.*

Evans, Tony, and Priscilla Shirer. *Prayers for Victory in Spiritual Warfare.*

Keller, Timothy. *Prayer: Experiencing Awe and Intimacy with God.*

Lewis, C. S. *How to Pray.*

McRoberts, Justin, and Scott Erickson. *Prayer: Forty Days of Practice.*

Moore, Beth. *Praying God's Word: Breaking Free from Spiritual Strongholds.*

Omartian, Stormie. *The Power of a Praying Mom.*

———. *The Power of a Praying Wife.*

————. *The Power of a Praying Woman.*

Shirer, Priscilla. *Fervent: A Woman's Battle Plan to Serious, Specific, and Strategic Prayer.*

Sorge, Bob. *Secrets of the Secret Place.*

Yancey, Philip. *Prayer: Does It Make Any Difference?*

Young, Sarah. *Jesus Calling: Enjoying Peace in His Presence.*

ACKNOWLEDGMENTS

This book started out as daily posts on Instagram. The journey of these words from social media into a physical book happened only because numerous people encouraged me to do so. Thank you, Chanda Stegall and Monique Jennings, for encouraging me to take these words farther than the internet. Your efforts to figure out how to put them on paper are the reason so many more people will deepen their connection with God through prayer. I'm also so grateful for Margot Starbuck, a talented writer who not only is a rock star with her own words but also has done a wonderful job taking mine and making them better. Thanks to my dear friend Vornadette Simpson and intern Catherine Fitzgerald, who have pored over this book multiple times to make sure the content is communicated with excellence. Every word you suggested and edited is appreciated. Thank you to the rest of my 2020 intern team—Brittanie Joyner, Dana Lapish, Debbie Mason, Deitra Baker, Kayla Thomas, Kristy Floyd, and Marissa Moore—who lent some of their own prayers so that readers of this book can have a starting point for their own prayer journeys.

Thank you to the Zondervan team, who willingly accepted the idea for this project and worked hard to bring it to the finish line while also extending kindness and grace to me during a difficult season. I'm so very grateful for Carolyn McCready, Tom Dean,

Bridgette Brooks, David Morris, Trinity McFadden, Brian Phipps, and the rest of the team for providing encouragement and support. It has been a privilege to partner with you.

Thank you to my husband, Jessie, and the three of our children who are still at home—Tre', Kanaan, and Joel. You have made room for me to get this project done amid one of the most trying times of our lives, and I'm grateful for the gracious way you support me in my quest to help others. It is my honor to be a witness to your lives and to have the opportunity to make prayer for you a priority.

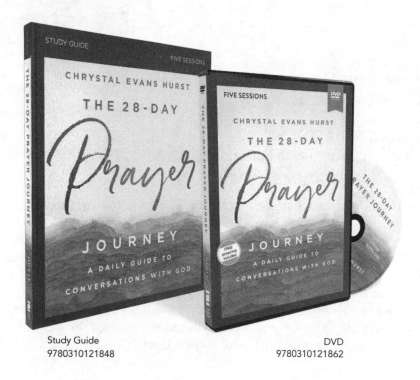